THE LION BOOK OF

1000

PRAYERS

for children

In memory of my father

THE LION BOOK OF
1000
PRAYERS
for children

Written and compiled by Lois Rock
Illustrated by Ruth Rivers

LION
CHILDREN'S

Written and compiled by Lois Rock
Illustrations copyright © 2003 Ruth Rivers
This edition copyright © 2010 Lion Hudson

The moral rights of the author and illustrator
have been asserted

A Lion Children's Book
an imprint of
Lion Hudson plc
Wilkinson House, Jordan Hill Road,
Oxford OX2 8DR, England
www.lionhudson.com
ISBN 978 0 7459 6231 3

First edition 2003
This revised edition 2010
10 9 8 7 6 5 4 3 2 1

A catalogue record for this book is available
from the British Library

Typeset in 11/14 Baskerville BT
Printed in China February 2011 (manufacturer LH06)

Distributed by:
UK: Marston Book Services Ltd, PO Box 269, Abingdon,
Oxon OX14 4YN
USA: Trafalgar Square Publishing, 814 N Franklin Street,
Chicago, IL 60610
USA Christian Market: Kregel Publications, PO Box 2607,
Grand Rapids, MI 49501

Contents

1 A New Day

1 **On this New Day**

Dearest God,
on this new day,
listen to me
as I pray.

Dearest God,
the day is new:
help me in
the things I do.

2 **Prayer for the Morning**

O God,
I will pray to you in the morning,
I will pray to you at sunrise.

I will ask you to show me the way that
I should go.

I will ask you to protect me from the people
who do not like me, who want to hurt me.

I will trust in you to protect me,
I will trust in your love.

From Psalm 5

3 Morning Fires

Angels have lit the morning fires,
The clouds are glowing pink;
The blue smoke rises in the sky,
And night's grey ashes sink.

4 Come into My Soul

Come into my soul, Lord,
as the dawn breaks into the sky;
let your sun rise in my heart
at the coming of the day.

Traditional

5 Time to Pray

Now is the gentle, joyful morning
Now is the break of day
Now is the time the sun comes shining
Now is the time to pray.

6 Holy God!

Holy, holy, holy, Lord God Almighty!
Early in the morning our song shall rise
to thee.

Bishop Herbert (1782–1826)

7 Quiet Whispers of God

I am listening in the stillness
for the quiet whispers of creation
that tell me where God is moving
in the clear blue morning.

8 The Angel of the Morning

God has wrapped this summer day like
a surprise present. God has wrapped it in
the soft white mist of morning. But look:
an angel has untied the ribbons of golden
sunlight, and there is the day... a perfect
clear blue day, for me.

9 Dawn is breaking

Dawn is breaking
silver with birdsong
like heaven awakening.

10 Pippa's Song

The year's at the spring,
And day's at the morn;
Morning's at seven;
The hill-side's dew-pearled;
The lark's on the wing;
The snail's on the thorn:
God's in his heaven –
All's right with the world!

Robert Browning (1812–89)

11 Quietly, in the Morning

Quietly, in the morning,
I rise and look at the sky
To watch the darkness scatter
As sunlight opens the sky.
The day lies clear before me,
All fresh and shining and new,
And then I ask God to guide me
In all that I have to do.

12 A Day Full of Promises

This day is full of promises
of everything that's good;
help me face its challenges
and do the things I should.

13 For this New Morning

For this new morning and its light,
For rest and shelter of the night,
For health and food, for love and friends,
For every gift your goodness sends,
We thank you, gracious Lord.

Anonymous

14 The New Morning

God has baptized the day
in the dark waters of night;
and now it rises clean and shining,
bright with the gold light of heaven.

Let us step bravely into this new day,
determined to walk the way of goodness,
  as God's children
under God's heaven.

HELP US THROUGH THIS DAY

15 Prayer for Happiness

God, who hast folded back the mantle
  of the night
to clothe us in the golden glory of the day,
chase from our hearts all gloomy thoughts
and make us glad with the brightness of
  hope.

Ancient collect

16 Kindliness and Cheerfulness

Dear God,
Help me to brighten this day with
kindliness and cheerfulness.

17 So Much to Do

O God,
There is so much to do today.
Help me to deal with each task, one by one.

18 Help Us to Do Good

Dear Lord Jesus, we shall have this day
only once; before it is gone, help us to
do all the good we can, so that today
is not a wasted day.

Stephen Grellet (1773–1855)

19 The Words I Say

May the words I say be kind,
May the words I say be true,
May the words I say be good,
May the words I say be few.

20 The Power of God

I bind unto myself today
The Power of God to hold and lead,
His eye to watch, his might to stay,
His ear to harken to my need;
The wisdom of my God to teach,
His hand to guide, his shield to ward;
The word of God to give me speech,
His heavenly host to be my guard.

St Patrick (389–461)

21 Morning Resolution

May I be a blessing to someone today,
and may someone be a blessing to me.

22 This New Day

This new day is for living,
This new day is for caring,
This new day is for giving,
This new day is for sharing.

23 Morning Thanks

Thanks be to thee, O Lord Jesus Christ,
for all the benefits which thou hast won
   for us,
for all the pains and insults which thou
   hast borne for us.
O most merciful Redeemer, Friend
   and Brother,
may we know thee more clearly,
love thee more dearly,
and follow thee more nearly,
day by day.

Richard of Chichester (1197–1253)

24 God's Sunlight

The sky may be blue
Or the sky may be grey:
We walk in God's sunlight
Through every day.

25 Help Me Through this Day

O God,
help me through this day.
May I do good to all those I meet,
through the things I say,
through the prayers I pray,
through the life I live.

26 Yesterday's Mistakes

Dear God,
Help me to learn from yesterday's mistakes.

27 Prayer for Knowledge

Let this day, O Lord, add some knowledge
or good deed to yesterday.

Lancelot Andrewes (1555–1626)

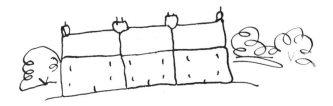

28 Can it Be Morning?

This is my "can-it-be-morning?" prayer, Lord,
the sort that I say from my bed;
I feel too tired to do good things today,
so may I just stay here instead?

29 A Hard Day Ahead

The day that lies before us will be hard,
and there is much that will distress us.
But we are determined,
with God's help,
to speak kindly,
to act generously,
and to forgive ourselves and others
any careless mistakes.

30 Prayer for Help Through the Day

Lord,
Help me to live this day
Quietly, easily.
Help me to lean upon Thy
Great strength
Trustfully, restfully,
To wait for the unfolding
Of Thy will
Patiently, serenely,
To meet others
Peacefully, joyously,
To face tomorrow
Confidently, courageously.

Amen

St Francis of Assisi (1181–1226)

BE WITH US

31 Do Not Forget Me

O Lord, thou knowest how busy I must
  be this day.
If I forget thee, do not thou forget me.

Sir Jacob Astley (before the battle of Edgehill, 1642)

32 A Second Chance

The morning is a good time to make a new
start; but, God, if I make mistakes, let me
make another new start in the afternoon.

33 A Message for Today

O let us feel you very near
When we kneel down to pray.
Let us be still that you may send
A message for today.

Anonymous

34 I Want to Stay in Bed

I wake up and I hear the sound
Of wind and storm and rain;
Dear God, I want to stay in bed
And fall asleep again.

Dear God, help me on stormy days
To rise and face the gale,
And make me brave and cheerful
So my courage does not fail.

35 In the Rush and Noise of Life

In the rush and noise of life, as you have
intervals, step within yourselves and be
still. Wait upon God and feel his good
presence; this will carry through your
day's business.

William Penn (1644–1718)

36 A Washing Prayer

O God, I have washed the outside of me,
Will you make me clean within,
To walk this whole day in righteousness
Untouched by the stain of sin.

37 Lord be with Us

Lord, be with us this day.
Within us to purify us;
Above us to draw us up;
Beneath us to sustain us;
Before us to lead us;
Behind us to restrain us;
Around us to protect us.

St Patrick (389–461)

38 A Voyage into the Unknown

The seas I must sail today, dear Lord,
I never have sailed before;
I trust in your all-encompassing grace
To bring me to evening's shore.

39 I Go Forth Today

I go forth today
in the might of heaven,
in the brightness of the sun,
in the whiteness of snow,
in the splendour of fire,
in the speed of lightning,
in the swiftness of wind,
in the firmness of rock.
I go forth today
in the hand of God.

Irish prayer (8th century)

40 The Little Things

God be in the little things of all I do today
So at the end the whole may be perfect in
every way.

41 Sunrise to Sunset

Bless the day, dear God, from sunrise
to sunset.
Bless the night, dear God, from sunset
to sunrise.

42 Beginning and Ending

Dear God,
Be with us in all we begin, and help us
bring everything to a good ending.

2 For the Very Young

43 A Day for Everything

This is a day for walking tall
This is a day for feeling small
This is a day for lots of noise
This is a day for quiet toys
This is a day to shout and sing
This is a day for everything.

44 This New Day

I wake
I wash
I dress
I say:
"Thank you
God
for this
new day."

HERE I AM

45 What Shall I Wear Today?

Dear God,
What shall I wear today?
If I were dressing up like a guardian angel,

I would wear clean underwear and clean
outerwear and clean socks and clean shoes
and I would make sure I stayed clean all
day; except for mud and stuff, which even
guardian angels know doesn't really matter.

46 Waking the Sun

I think the sun must have fallen asleep
Under a blanket of cloud;
Do you think, God, we could wake the
    sun up,
If we both shout very loud?

47 Someone Looking Upwards

God, look down from heaven:
Here on earth you'll see
Someone looking upwards –
That someone is me.

48 No One Quite the Same

God, do you remember me?
Do you still know my name?
Of course you do, 'cos I am me:
there's no one quite the same.

49 Never Forget Me

Your sky is so big
and I am so small.
Never forget me,
never at all.

50 God's Little Child

Here I am
in the great big world
with everywhere to explore;
and God made me
to live as his child
and love him for evermore.

51 If I Were an Angel

If I were an angel
then I would wear white
and only do things
that I knew to be right.

I'd put on a halo
of glittering gold
and I would be gentle
and I would be bold.

I'd fly through the sky
on my soft feathered wings
and tell all the people
of Jesus the king.

52 Keep Me Safe

God, my life has just begun;
keep me safe, your little one.

53 Growing to the Light

A little seed
unfolds its leaves
and grows up to the light;
and I will lift
my face to heaven
and learn to do what's right.

54 Doing Good in Little Things

Dear God,
Help me to do good
in the little things that I am allowed to do
so I will know how to do good
when I am allowed to do bigger things.

55 Who Made the Sun?

Who made the sun?
Who made the day?
Who made the hours
for work and play?

God made them all,
God made them good,
God helps us live
the way we should.

56 I Wash My Hands

I wash my hands
to make them clean
and ready to do good.

And God above
will teach me how
to do the things I should.

57 Hands

Hands to work
and hands to play,
hands to help
in every way.

Hands to clap
and hands to pray,
hands to praise God
every day.

58 Helping Hands

May my hands be helping hands
For all that must be done
That fetch and carry, lift and hold
And make the hard jobs fun.

May my hands be clever hands
In all I make and do
With sand and dough and clay and things
With paper, paint and glue.

May my hands be gentle hands
And may I never dare
To poke and prod and hurt and harm
But touch with love and care.

59 Words

Words can make us happy
Words can make us sad
Words can leave us feeling calm
WORDS CAN MAKE US MAD!
So we must be careful
In the things we say
Dear God, help us choose the words
That we use today.

60 When I Am in a Temper

When I am in a temper
When I get really mad
I can be very dangerous
I can be very bad.

I'm wild as a tiger
I'm wild as a bear
I'm wilder than a wildebeest
And I don't even care.

Dear God who made the tiger
Dear God who made the bear
Please let me know you love me still
And that you'll always care.

Mark Robinson

61 When it All Goes Wrong

Dear God,
I want so much to be good,
but sometimes I bubble over with excitement
and it all goes wrong.

Dear God,
I want so much to be good,
but sometimes I explode with temper
and it all goes wrong.

Dear God,
Put me back together again
and help me to begin again.

62 Oops!

Accidents will happen, Lord,
And things that spill will stain
So help me not to have
These silly accidents again.

MY FAMILY

63 For Baby

Prayer number one is for baby
Prayer number two is for me
Prayer number three is for everyone
Who's part of my family tree.

64 Patience

May our baby
stop that wailing
for I feel
my patience failing.

65 Sleepy Baby

Sleepy Baby
Do you know
Why God put us
Here below?

Nor do I
But hand in hand
We can try
To understand.

66 For Mummy

Dear God,
Take care of Mummy,
who takes good care of me,
and may our home be full of love
that all the world can see.

67 For Daddy

Bless my Dad,
so strong and tall:
the kindest Daddy
of them all.

68 God Bless Mummy

God bless Mummy when we're together
and when we are far away;
God bless her when she's busy at work,
and please give her time to play.

69 Brothers and Sisters

God bless my brother
and make him good
and help him do
the things he should.

God bless my sister
and make her good
and help her do
the things she should.

And God bless me
and make me good
and help me do
the things I should.

70 Me and Gran

Me and Gran
and Gran and me
are part of God's
big family.

71 For All the People Who Love Me

Bless all the people who love me, dear God,
and bless all the people I love;
help us to help one another each day
and make earth like heaven above.

72 Kind People

Thank you, dear God,
for the many kind people
who help us along our way,
who smile when we're happy,
who care when we're tearful,
who keep us safe all through the day.

OUT AND ABOUT

73 As We Go Out

God keep us safe as we go out
Just Mum and baby and me
May we have everything we need
and may we walk cheerfully.

74 Grown-up and Child Prayer

Today we will go somewhere new together:
God, help us find the way.

And then we will say goodbye:
God, help us both to be brave.

And then we will each do something
     different:
God, help us to do that something well.

And then we will meet again:
God, make the time come quickly,
so we can be together
and tell the other all about what we
     have done.

75 Looking for a Place to Park

Bless our visit
to this place.
Help us find
a parking space
big enough
to take our car,
somewhere safe
and not too far.

76 Until We Meet Again

God take care of everyone
Until we meet again
Keep us safe through sun and snow
And wind and hail and rain.

77 Ready for All Kinds of Weather

Ready for sun
and ready for rain
and ready for all kinds of weather;
ready to hold
the hand of God
as we all go out together.

78 Muddy Boots

For my bright and shiny boots
I give you thanks, O God;
and thank you
for the very muddy places where I trod.

79 A Windy Day

Bless our fingers, bless our toes,
When the wind so blustery blows.
Keep us warm in boots and gloves,
Wrap us in your kindly love.

80 Winter Clothes

Winter boots for puddles
Winter boots for snow
Winter boots for all the muddy
    places that I go.

Winter hats for chilly days
Winter hats for storms
Thank you, God, for winter clothes
    that help to keep us warm.

81 Our Special Day

God, please take great care of us
on this, our special day.
Please, God, send the golden sun
and blow the rain away.

May we all stay very safe,
and may we all have fun.
Now we have to hurry, God,
our great day has begun.

82 A Day at the Seaside

A day of sun
A day of fun
A day of sand and sea

A day to thank
the God of fun
for taking care of me.

Our World

83 Food to Share

Let us say
A thank you prayer
For the food
That's here to share.

84 Little Deeds of Kindness

Little deeds of kindness,
Little words of love,
Help to make earth happy,
Like the heaven above.

Julia Carney (1823–1908)

85 Baby Pets

Baby creatures, just awakened,
You are part of God's creation;
Baby creatures, oh, so small,
God is father of us all.

86 Sowing Seeds

Here are the seeds
   we plan to sow;
bless them, dear God,
   and make them grow.

QUIET TIMES

87 On a Gloomy Day

Today seems rather gloomy
Today seems rather slow
Today I don't know what to do
Or where I want to go.

Today is a time for thinking
Today is a time to sigh
And just be glad I'm here with you
Beneath God's bright blue sky.

88 Please Make Things Better

Dear God,
This is a sad day.
This is a day filled with tears.
This is the sort of day that only you
   can mend, dear God.
Please come and make things better.

89 Be a Friend to Me

Jesus, friend of little children,
   Be a friend to me;
Take my hand, and ever keep me
   Close to thee.

Never leave me, nor forsake me;
   Ever be my friend;
For I need thee, from life's dawning
   To its end.

Walter J. Mathams (1851–1931)

90 Wriggly

May God bless all things wriggly
As wriggly as can be
Like worms and snakes and tadpoles
And, most of all, bless me.

91 Be Still

Feet! Be still.
We're going to pray.

Hands! Be still.
We're going to pray.

You! Be still.
And me! Be still.

God wants to hear what we say.

92 God's Love and Care

Help us to remember
All your love and care,
Trust in you and love you,
Always, everywhere.

W. St Hill Bourne (1846–1929)

93 God Be Everywhere

Shadows in the hallway
Shadows on the stair
God be always near me
God be everywhere.

94 Come Near

Here I am, God,
crouching small.

Here I am God,
standing tall.

Now I'm jumping
like a clown.

Now I'm still
and sitting down.

Now I'm praying:
can you hear?

If you can, dear God,
come near.

95 Prayers 1–10

This is my prayer number 1:
bless the day that's just begun.

This is my prayer number 2:
may the sky be clear and blue.

This is my prayer number 3:
God, please take good care of me.

This is my prayer number 4:
help me love you more and more.

This is my prayer number 5:
make me glad to be alive.

This is my prayer number 6:
help me when I'm in a fix.

This is my prayer number 7:
make this world a bit like heaven.

This is my prayer number 8:
put an end to hurt and hate.

This is my prayer number 9:
let the light of kindness shine.

This is my prayer number 10:
bring me safe to bed again.

GOOD NIGHT

96 God Bless the Moon

I see the moon
And the moon sees me;
God bless the moon
And God bless me.

Traditional

97 A Silver Moon

A silver moon
A velvet sky:
May the angels
Watch close by.

A velvet sky
A silver moon:
May I fall asleep
Quite soon.

98 Tucked Up in Bed

Wrap me in a snuggly quilt
and tuck me into bed.
Keep me in a cosy house,
a roof above my head.

Let the world spin round about
till we can see the sun
and know when it is morning
and the new day has begun.

99 For People Everywhere

Tucked up in my little bed,
I say a little prayer
For all the people in this house
And people everywhere.

Sophie Piper

100 Close Your Eyes

Hands together, close your eyes,
Pray to God above
That the night be filled with peace,
And the day with love.

Sophie Piper

3 All About Me

101 Truly Me

Each and every day
this prayer, dear Lord, I pray:
make me wise to see
whom I should truly be.

102 A Dream for Our Lives

Dear God,
Give each one of us a dream for our lives
so that we may become truly ourselves.

FEELING LOVED

103 A Child of God

I looked into a silver pond
and there I saw a face:
a child of God looked up at me
with kindliness and grace.

104 God Has Counted Me

God has counted the stars in the
   heavens,
God has counted the leaves on the tree;
God has counted the children on earth:
I know God has counted me.

105 God Cares for Me

God, who made the earth,
The air, the sky, the sea,
Who gave the light its birth,
Careth for me.

God, who made the grass,
The flower, the fruit, the tree,
The day and night to pass,
Careth for me.

God, who made all things,
On earth, in air, in sea,
Who changing seasons brings,
Careth for me.

Sarah Betts Rhodes (c. 1870)

106 Safe in God's Love

There is no place where God is not –
wherever I go, there God is.
Now and always he upholds me with
　his power
and keeps me safe in his love.

Anonymous

107 Not a Little Angel

Dear God,
When I was little
people called me a little angel,
but now I'm older
and they realize they were mistaken.

Dear God,
Please find a place in your love
for someone who is a chatterbox,
a nuisance and a troublemaker.

Amen

108 Growing in Goodness

Teach me how to grow in goodness.

Walter J. Mathams (1853–1931)

109 Believe in Yourself

Believe in yourself and think well of others;
Believe in others and show them your love;
Believe in the greatness beyond all knowing:
Within and beyond, below and above.

110 Being Grateful

Thou who hast given so much to me
Give one thing more, a grateful heart,
    for Christ's sake.

George Herbert (1593–1632)

Feeling Insecure

111 **Afraid**

Dear God,
No one seems to understand why I feel
so scared to be out on my own...
at school, at play, just walking.

Don't they know how afraid I am
of getting lost...
so lost that I might never find myself again.

Please send kind people to help me,
and angels to guide me and wrap your love
all around me.

Amen

112 **Outside**

When I feel left out of a circle of friends
I shall put my trust in the circle of God's love.

113 Hesitant and Uncertain

Father,
I am seeking:
I am hesitant and uncertain,
but will you, O God,
watch over each step of mine
and guide me.

St Augustine (354–430)

114 Happy to Be Me

Dear God,
Make me happy to be me, not disappointed
that I'm not someone else.

115 Treated Badly

Dear God,
I know I am being treated badly by people
who ought to be taking care of me.

Dear God,
Make it easy for me to tell someone
who can help.

116 May I Be Glad

May I be glad that I walk like me.
May I be glad that I talk like me.
May I be glad that I act like me.
May I be glad that I look like me.

May I be glad to be young like me.
May I be glad to grow old like me.
May I be glad to live life as me.
May I be glad to face God as me.

117 Special Love

Dear God,
I am so very ordinary
I need your very special love.

118 Changing

Dear God,
Please welcome me as I am
and then begin changing me for the better.

119 Growing Wiser

I pray for the person I see in the mirror,
who's really a lot like me;
who needs to grow older and wiser
  and kinder
to be the best they can be.

120 A Useful Life

Dear God,
Make my life useful
even though I sometimes feel useless.

121 The Angry Beast Inside

O God,
There is an angry beast inside me.
It wants to fight and it likes to hurt.
It likes to feel strong and powerful.
It wants to be a winner.

And why should I not let it out?
Why should I not fight and hurt?
Why should I not feel strong and powerful?
Why should I be a loser?

O God,
What is that you are saying?
Speak louder.

122 Love Me When I'm Bad

Dear God, who made volcanoes,
Love me when I'm angry.

Dear God, who made glaciers,
Love me when I'm cruel.

Dear God, who made marshlands,
Love me when I'm gloomy.

Dear God, who made mudflats,
Love me when I'm sulking.

123 Staying Out of Trouble

Dear God,
Whenever I get into trouble,
I like drinking water
because I've noticed
you almost never get told off
for drinking water.

Dear God,
Whenever I get into trouble,
I like breathing air
because I've noticed
you almost never get told off
for breathing air.

Dear God,
Whenever I get into trouble,
I like standing on solid ground
because I've noticed
you almost never get told off
for standing on solid ground.

Dear God,
Whenever I get into trouble,
I like gazing at the setting sun
because I've noticed
you almost never get told off
for gazing at the setting sun.

THE THINGS OF EVERY DAY

124 Things that Matter

Dear God,
I will try to care about the things that
matter to you; will you please show how
much you care about the things that
matter to me?

125 **Bad Hair Day**

Dear God,
I know you do not judge people by outward
appearances; if you did, you wouldn't have
given us hair with a mind of its own.

126 **Poor Old Me**

In heaven, they say, we will all have a new
body and shining robes.

But, God, it would be more useful to have
the body and clothes here and now, where
appearances really seem to matter.

127 **Bad Shoes**

O God,
How can I go out in shoes like these?
I didn't choose them. I don't like them.
I didn't ask my parents to spend their
hard-earned money on them.

O God,
Please help me get through the day as
invisibly as possible, and may the shoes
fall apart very soon.

128 Advice

Kind Jesus,
Do you still remember what it's like to
be growing up on earth? Do you have any
advice for those of us still suffering here
below?

129 Lost Keys

O God, we can't go out,
We cannot find our keys,
My mother's getting panicky,
Oh, let me find them, please.

130 The Gap in My Mouth

Dear God,
Please bless the gap in my mouth
It's been there for quite some while.

Dear God,
Please bless the tooth that will grow
And give me a cheerful smile.

131 Look How I Have Grown

All around the seasons
another year has flown.
Now it is my birthday
and look how I have grown
all around the seasons
to celebrate this day
with everyone who loves me
and God to guide my way.

132 My Birthday

Thank you for the year gone by
and all that I have done.
Thank you for my birthday
and the year that is to come.

133 Things

Dear God,
Thank you for the things I have
  in abundance,
to enjoy with frivolity.

Thank you for the things of which
  I have enough,
to enjoy thoughtfully.

Thank you for the things that I lack
that keep me trusting in your
 many blessings.

Sophie Piper

GOD BY MY SIDE

134 God Be in My Head

God be in my head, and in my
 understanding;
God be in my eyes, and in my looking;
God be in my mouth, and in my speaking;
God be in my heart, and in my thinking;
God be at my end, and at my departing.

Old Sarum primer (1527)

135 Christ Be with Me

Christ be with me
Christ within me
Christ behind me
Christ before me
Christ beside me
Christ to win me

Christ to comfort and restore me
Christ beneath me
Christ above me
Christ in quiet and
Christ in danger
Christ in hearts of all that love me
Christ in mouth of friend and stranger.

St Patrick (389–461)

136 Be in All that I Do

Dear God,
Be in all that I do, now and always.

Victoria Tebbs

137 In My Heart

Lord, I want to be a Christian
  in-na my heart
  in-na my heart
Lord, I want to be a Christian
  in-na my heart
  in-na my heart
In-na my heart
  in-na my heart
Lord, I want to be a Christian
  in-na my heart.

Lord, I want to be more loving
  in-na my heart
  in-na my heart...

Lord, I want to be like Jesus
  in-na my heart
  in-na my heart
Lord, I want to be like Jesus
  in-na my heart
  in-na my heart
In-na my heart
  in-na my heart
Lord, I want to be like Jesus
  in-na my heart.

Black spiritual

138 Gentleness and Simplicity

Take from me, O Lord God, all pride and
vanity, all boasting and self-assertion, and
give me the true courage that shows itself
in gentleness; the true vision that shows
itself in simplicity; and the true power
that shows itself in modesty: through
Jesus Christ our Lord.

Charles Kingsley (1819–75)

139 Close to Me

Dear God,
Let me remember you are always close
to me, with your hand outstretched in
case I need to hold on to you.

Victoria Tebbs

140 Always by My Side

Thank you for your everlasting love.
Thank you for always being by my side.

Victoria Tebbs

4 People I Love

141 God Bless All Those that I Love

God bless all those that I love;
God bless all those that love me;
God bless all those that love those that
  I love,
And all those that love those that love me.

From an old New England sampler

142 All People in God's Care

We commend unto you, O Lord,
our souls and our bodies,
our minds and our thoughts,
our prayers and our hopes,
our health and our work,
our life and our death,
our parents and brothers and sisters,
our benefactors and friends,
our neighbours, our countrymen,
and all Christian folk,
this day and always.

Lancelot Andrewes (1555–1626)

FAMILIES

143 Bless My Family

Dear God, bless all my family,
as I tell you each name;
and please bless each one differently
for no one's quite the same.

144 A Prayer for Baby

I say a prayer for Baby –
"God help you and God bless,
God guard you and God guide you
With love and gentleness."

145 Sleepless Nights

Baby was crying and
Mummy was weeping
All through the night
When they should have been sleeping.

I think our baby
Is one of the best
But, O God, it's time
That we all had some rest.

146 Let Me Be Me

Dear God,
Let my brother be my brother
and let me be me.

Let my sister be my sister
and let me be me.

Let us all be who we are
and let us all grow to be better and kinder.

147 Feeling Special

O God,
It's not easy being the eldest child. There
are so many things you have to do first.

O God,
It's not easy being the youngest child. There
are so many things you only get to do last.

O God,
It's not easy being a middle child. You have
to keep thinking of new ways of being either
first or last at something.

O God,
May all children feel special, wherever they
fit in the family.

148 Held Together with Love

Thank you, dear God,
for putting me in a family that is
   held together with love.

149 When Parents Are Angry

Dear God,
Be a kind father to me,
especially when my dad is in a temper.

Dear God,
Be a gentle mother to me,
especially when my mum is in a rage.

150 Coping with Worry

My mother lives in the shadow of worry.

Dear God,
Lead her into the sunshine of happiness.

151 Understanding Each Other

Help parents to understand their children.
Help children to understand their parents.

From Ephesians 6:1–4

152 Praying

Dear God,
I want to pray what my dad would pray if
he wasn't so busy.

I want to pray what my mum would pray if
she wasn't so tired.

I want to pray what my brother would pray
if he wasn't glued to the screen.

I want to pray what my sister would pray if
she wasn't dancing to music.

These are my prayers, dear God; will you
please tell me the words.

153 Hearing Wise Things

Dear God,
Help me to hear the wise things
   my mother says.
Help me to hear the wise things
   my father says.

154 Generations Talking

Dear God,
Help me to listen to my gran
and make the most of being young.

Help my gran to listen to me
and learn to enjoy every birthday.

155 God Bless Grandad

God bless Grandad
through the bright blue day.
God bless Grandad
through the dark grey night.
God bless Grandad
when we hug together.
God bless Grandad
when we're out of sight.

156 Near and Far Away

God bless my mum, dear God,
when I am near to her
and when I am far away.

God bless my dad, dear God,
when I am near to him
and when I am far away.

Please bless me, dear God,
when I feel near to you
and when I feel far away.

157 Aunties with Kisses

Save me from aunties with kisses
who shriek when they see how I've grown;
help me to smile politely
and stifle the longing to moan.

Save me from uncles with wrinkles
who act like they're younger than me;
help me to act like an angel
when relatives come round for tea.

158 Distant Relatives

God bless my distant relatives who send me
presents; even though I may not want their
gifts, they make me feel love is all around.

Victoria Tebbs

159 People Who Don't Say Prayers

Dear God,
This is a prayer asking you to help the
people I love who don't say prayers. They
never say they love you, but we love them
and we love you.

160 What Family Means

May family mean fun.

May family mean friends.

May family mean forgiveness.

May family mean for ever.

161 Keep Us Together

O God,
When family relationships are falling apart,
please keep each one of us together.

162 Cautious Thanks

In all the times we've loved and laughed
And fought and rowed and hated
We give a cautious thanks for those
To whom we are related.

163 At Home with Myself

Dear God,
Sometimes I don't feel at home with
   my family;
please help me to feel at home with myself.

164 Circle of Love

Dear God,
We gather here in a family circle.
We were not always family,
But we are becoming family.
Hold us in the circle of your love.

165 Love and Hate

Dear God,
Help me to love the people in my family
even when I hate them.

166 Togetherness

Dear God,
May this family be a place of togetherness
that supports us when we go out alone.

167 For Those Who Love Me

I live for those who love me,
   Whose hearts are kind and true;
For the heaven that smiles above me,
   And awaits my spirit too;
For all human ties that bind me,
For the task my God assigned me,
For the bright hopes left behind me,
   And the good that I can do.

George Linnaeus Banks (1821–81)

168 A Place of Kindness and Forgiveness

Bless all our families, dear God.
May they be a place of kindness and
forgiveness, where everyone can learn
to be truly themselves.

169 Thanks for My Family

I give thanks for the people
who are my home:
we share a place to shelter;
we share our food;
we share our times of work
and play and rest;
we share our lives.

FRIENDS

170 Being a Good Friend

Dear God,
Help me to be a good friend to myself
so I can learn to be a good friend to others.

Help me to be kind to myself
so I can learn to be kind to others.

Help me to forgive myself
so I can learn to forgive others.

Help me to love myself
so I can learn to love others.

171 Sitting Down with Friends

Dear God,
May we sit down with friends through
   all our days:
On the plastic chairs of playgroup,
On the wooden chairs at school,
On the soft and sagging sofas of home,
On the folding chairs of holidays,
On the fashionable seats of restaurants
And on the dusty seats in the garden
Till at last, when we have grown old,
We need our friends to help us in
   and out of chairs.

172 Choosing Friends Wisely

Dear God,
Help me to make good friends
who make it easy for me to be a
   good person.
Help me to walk away from bad friends
who make it easy for me to be a bad person.

173 Thank You for My Friends

Dear God,
Thank you for my friends.
Help me to be a good friend to others.

174 Befriending

We
not me.

Share
not tear.

Mend
not end

and so
befriend.

175 Left Out

Dear God,
I'm feeling all left out. Help me to be brave
about being alone.

176 Being a Friend

Dear God,
Help me be kind to someone who feels left
out; everyone needs at least one friend.

Victoria Tebbs

177 Mending a Relationship

O God,
We were once enemies.
Now we promise to become friends.
Help us learn to respect one another.
Help us learn to trust one another.
Help us learn to be kind to one another.

178 Preserving Friendships

O God,
Help our battered friendships to survive.

179 Forgiving Friends

O God,
Help us to forgive our friends
when they let us down.

180 May Friendship Last

May friendship last
even when we are forgetful.

May friendship last
even when we are busy.

May friendship last
even when we are tired.

May friendship last.

181 Guard Our Friendships

Dear God,
guard our friendships:

Encourage us,
that we may encourage one another.

Inspire us,
that we may inspire one another.

Strengthen us,
that we may strengthen one another.

Remember us,
that we may remember one another.

Sophie Piper

5 At Home

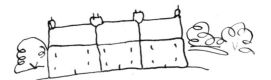

182 A Holy Place

Lord, make this house
a holy place
filled with your love
and heaven's grace.

183 My Home

Thank you, dear God, for the little place
that is my home – more special to me than
all the stars in the universe.

BLESS OUR HOME

184 A New Home

Dear God,
We have arrived
at this, our new home,
feeling as lost
as windblown seeds
that are dropped upon the earth.

Let us put down roots
here where we have landed,
and let our lives unfold
in your love and light.

185 Bless the Window

Bless the window
Bless the door
Bless the ceiling
Bless the floor
Bless this place which is our home
Bless us as we go and come.

186 Windows to the Sky

Our home is built firmly upon the earth
but its windows all look to the sky;
we live on this earth to bring blessings
    to all
beneath heaven's watchful eye.

187 A Happy Place

Dear God,
May our home be a happy place,
and may every happy place feel like home.

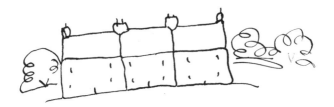

188 May Our Home Be Happy

May our home be happy
May our home be cosy
May our home be safe
May our home be blessed.

189 Safe at Home

A floor against the chill of earth
A roof against the sky
And walls against the rain and wind
To keep us safe and dry.

190 Protect Our Home

Save our home from rain and flood
and wind and gale and storm;
save our home from frost and snow
and keep us dry and warm.

191 Putting Things Away

O God, are there servants in heaven
Whose job is to put things away?
And can they be sent here to help us,
Kind Heavenly Father, I pray?

192 Mess

Bless the mess
but make us strong
to put things
where they belong.

193 A Welcoming Home

Dear God,
May our house be a place where all our
visitors can feel at home.

194 A Welcome for All

Dear God, bless those who visit us: family,
friends and strangers. May we make our
home a place of love and kindness for all.
May we share the things we have with
generosity and cheerfulness.

Victoria Tebbs

195 A Place of Love

O God,
make the door of this house wide enough
to receive all who need human love and
fellowship, and a heavenly Father's care;
and narrow enough to shut out
all envy, pride and hate.
Make its threshold smooth enough
to be no stumbling block to children,
nor to straying feet,
but rugged enough to turn back
the tempter's power:
make it a gateway
to thine eternal kingdom.

Bishop Thomas Ken (1637–1711)

196 A Home of Light and Laughter

Dear Lord,
Please let our house be a home full of
love – a welcoming place for our family
and friends. May it be cosy and warm and
light – and brimming with laughter and joy.

Jenni Dutton

Bless Our Food

197 The Board is Spread

Morning is here,
The board is spread,
Thanks be to God,
Who gives us bread.

Anonymous

198 We Are Hungry

We are hungry,
We have food,
We are family,
God is good.

199 All Good Gifts Around Us

All good gifts around us,
  Are sent from heaven above,
Then thank the Lord, O thank the Lord,
  For all his love.

Matthias Claudius (1740–1815), translated by
Jane Montgomery Campbell (1817–78)

200 Daily Food

For health and strength
and daily food,
we praise your name,
O Lord.

Traditional

201 Let My Food Strengthen Me

Bless me, O Lord, and let my food
strengthen me to serve thee, for
Christ's sake.

Isaac Watts (1674–1748)

202 Be Present at Our Table

Be present at our table, Lord;
Be here and everywhere adored;
Thy Creatures bless and grant that we
May feast in Paradise with Thee.

John Cennick, Moravian deacon (1741)

203 Food of Goodness

Blessed are you, Lord our God, king of the
universe, who feeds the entire world in his
goodness – with grace, with kindness and
with mercy. He gives food to all life, for his
kindness is eternal… Blessed are you, God,
who nourishes all.

Jewish grace

204 Each Time We Eat

Each time we eat,
may we remember God's love.

Prayer from China

205 The Bread is Warm and Fresh

The bread is warm and fresh,
The water cool and clear.
Lord of all life, be with us,
Lord of all life, be near.

African grace

206 Some Hae Meat

Some hae meat, and canna eat,
 And some wad eat that want it;
But we hae meat, and we can eat,
 And sae the Lord be thankit.

The Selkirk Grace, Robert Burns (1759–96)

207 Thanks for Our Food

God is great, God is good,
Let us thank him for our food.

Traditional, used in the White House
by President Jimmy Carter

208 Good Food

The food is good
The food is hot
O Lord, we're glad
To eat the lot.

209 A Time for Sharing

This meal is time for caring
This meal is food for sharing.

210 The Gift of Food

We give thanks for our hunger,
We give thanks for our food,
We give thanks for enough of each
To do our bodies good.

211 Take a Moment

Let us take a moment
To thank God for our food,
For friends around the table
And everything that's good.

212 Remembering the Hungry

As we eat this delicious food, let us
remember those who do not have enough
to eat.

Victoria Tebbs

213 Eat with Thankfulness

Dear God,
May we eat this meal with thankfulness
And with the proper cutlery.

214 Food I Don't Like

Dear God,
There are many kinds of food I don't
like. Thank you that I have enough food
that I can choose things I do like.

Olwen Turchetta

215 For Chocolate-Lovers

God bless those who grow chocolate
God bless those who harvest chocolate
God bless those who manufacture chocolate
God bless those who transport chocolate
God bless those who sell chocolate
God bless those who eat chocolate.

May we who are a chocolate family
Treat one another as brothers and sisters.

216 The Cookie Jar Prayer

Dear God, who watches us from afar,
please turn your eyes from the cookie jar.
For I'm in need of a little snack
and once I start, there's no holding back.

217 A Sharing Rhyme

A lunch that's plenty for one
is also enough for two
and sharing is much more fun
so that is what we will do.

218 Let's Eat Now

We are hungry, dear Lord.
We are thirsty, dear Lord.
We are thankful, dear Lord.
So let's eat now, dear Lord.

6 At School

219 If Our School Were in Heaven

If our school were in heaven,
we would sweep the paths clean.

If our school were in heaven,
we would cultivate its garden.

If our school were in heaven,
we would keep our things neat.

If our school were in heaven,
we would display our work for the angels
 to see.

If our school were in heaven,
we would treat everyone as a child of God.

So here on earth we will do these things
and so make our school more like heaven.

220 Bless Our School

Dear God,
Bless our school.
Bless the buildings.
Bless the playground.
Bless the teachers and everyone
who works here.
Bless the helpers and everyone
who volunteers.
Bless the work we do.
Bless the games we play.
Bless each and every one of us.
May our school be a place of
happiness, respect and love.

221 After the Holidays

Dear God,
The holidays are over and we return to
school for a new year. May it be for us all
a new start: a chance to surprise ourselves
at what we can achieve, a new opportunity
to make friends and to make this school
a community where everyone can feel at
home.

222 Bless Our Classroom

Bless our classroom
and the place where we sit.

Bless our classroom
and the place where we listen.

Bless our classroom
and the place where we work.

Bless our classroom
and the place where we laugh.

Bless our classroom
and the place where we learn.

223 Bless to Me, O God...

Bless to me, O God,
the work of my hands.
Bless to me, O God,
the work of my mind.
Bless to me, O God,
the work of my heart.

Anonymous

224 A Really Good School

Dear God,
Let us make our school
a really good school:
let us be kind,
let us be fair,
let us be honest,
let us be respectful,
let us be friendly,
let us be ready to forgive,
let us grow up good.

OUT OF SCHOOL

225 School Trip

Dear God,
Take care of those who are going on
a school trip today.
May the arrangements all work out well.
May the weather be good.
May everyone be helpful to one another
and listen to one another.
May everyone take good care of one
another, so no one feels lost or anxious.
May everyone come home safely, with
exciting tales to tell of their adventures.

226 Travelling to School

Dear God,
Take care of everyone as they travel to
and from school. Keep them safe every day,
come winter, come summer.

227 For Those Who Are Unwell

Dear God,
We remember people who are not at school
today because they are unwell. May they
all be tucked up in a cosy place, with
everything they need to help them feel
better. May they be well again very soon.

LEARNING AT SCHOOL

228 New Things

Dear God,
Help us as we learn new things. If we learn
quickly and easily, may we help others to
understand. If we make mistakes, may we
understand what went wrong. Help us never
to be afraid of new things, but to see them
as an adventure.

229 Asking Questions

Dear God,
When I don't understand the things I am
taught at school, make me brave to ask
questions until I do.

230 Hard Lessons

Dear God,
Sometimes the things we have to do in
lessons seem too hard. Help me to get all
the easy things right, and only try the hard
things one little bit at a time.

231 May I Be a Blessing

Dear God,
May I be a blessing to the teachers at my
school, but may none of my friends notice.

232 Being Kind

Dear God,
May everyone I meet in school know they
can count on me to be kind.

233 Safe Playground

Dear God,
May the playground be a safe place:
no unkind games,
no unkind words,
no unkind looks.

234 Learning to Be Wise

We come to school not to learn to be clever,
but to learn to be wise.

235 A Fresh Beginning

Start each day with a fresh beginning;
as if this whole world was made anew.

Motto from an Amish school in Pennsylvania

236 Who Am I?

I am only me, but I'm still someone.
I cannot do everything, but I can
   do something.
Just because I cannot do everything does
   not give me the right to do nothing.

Motto from an Amish school in Pennsylvania

237 At Home in School

May everyone feel at home in this school:
at home in the classroom,
at home in the buildings,
at home in the playground,
at home with one another.

238 Bless this Day of Learning

Bless this day of learning:
this day of learning mathematics;
this day of learning science;
this day of learning games;
this day of learning crafts...

this day of learning honesty;
this day of learning responsibility;
this day of learning kindness;
this day of learning forgiveness.

239 Things We Pray For

The things, good Lord, that we pray for,
give us grace to work for; through Jesus
Christ our Lord.

Sir Thomas More (1478–1535)

240 For Dawn of Grey

For dawn of grey and tattered sky,
for silver rain on grass and tree;
for song and laughter and work well done,
our thankful hearts we raise to thee.

Anonymous

241 Stars

Dear God,
We have come to school not so much to
earn stars but to learn to be stars, each in
our own special way.

APPRECIATING LEARNING

242 Pictures

Dear God,
Teach me to paint so that every picture
I make is a song of praise to your creation.

243 The Beauty of Numbers

Thank you, dear God, for the beauty of
numbers that add up and calculations that
work out right.

244 Exploring God's World

Dear God,
The more I explore your world, the more
I marvel at your creation. It is a triumph
of science and engineering... and more than
that, it contains great mysteries that I am yet
to understand.

245 Using Words Well

Dear God,
Thank you for words.
Help us to use them well:
to say them clearly;
to write them carefully;
to spell them correctly;
to communicate effectively.

May we learn to use words well now so
that all through our lives we will be better
able to work for what is true and right
and honest.

246 The Beauty of Words

Dear God,
Thank you for the beauty of words.
Thank you for the clever way they tell
us facts.
Thank you for the poetic way they tell
us feelings.
Thank you for the mysterious way they
inspire faith.

DIFFICULT TIMES

247 The Important Test

This is an important test,
God help us to do our best.

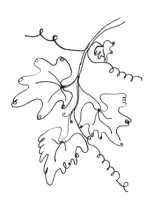

248 A Bad Day at School

I've had a bad day at school, dear God,
An ever so very bad day;
You'd hardly believe how bad it was:
Just take those bad memories away.

And then let me start again, dear God,
And may my tomorrow be good;
You've got to believe how hard I'll try
To do all the things that I should.

249 An Unfair Day at School

Dear God,
Being told off at school for something I did
not do may not seem very important, but
it is very important to me. It is like a little
weed of unfairness that will grow up into a
huge plant and smother all the earth. Dear
God, should I let this little unfairness go
by, or should I go back tomorrow and make
people understand what really happened?
Dear God, make me wise to know how to
uproot all unfairness so that what is true
and right may clearly be seen.

250 No Gold Star

Dear God,
I tried my best with my schoolwork,
but it didn't get 10 out of 10.
It didn't get an A grade.
It didn't win a gold star.

Dear God,
I want to believe that even now
my guardian angel
is pinning up a gold star in heaven
just because you and all the angels
are glad that I'm me.

251 Help Me to Learn to Get Things Right

Dear God, my head is hurting,
Dear God, my brain is dead,
Dear God, I didn't understand
    a thing the teacher said.

Dear God, I'm not too clever,
Dear God, I'm not that bright,
Dear God, please help me find a way
    to learn to get things right.

252 Enemies

Enemies are awful
and enemies are mean
but all their wicked, wicked deeds
by God above are seen.
Now God is all forgiving
but God is also good
and God will sort them out one day
just like I wish I could.

253 Bullies Say...

Bullies:
They say, "We're only teasing."
But it's not a joke to me.

They say, "We're only playing."
But it's not a game to me.

They say, "We don't mean anything nasty."
But O God, that's not true.
That's not true.

254 The Silent Cry

I dare not say anything
about the things that frighten me,
about the people who hurt me,
about how I get pushed around.

But now I am telling my silent nothing
so it can be shouted aloud in heaven –
aloud, aloud, aloud, aloud:
till someone on earth hears my cry.

255 Bullies

The bullies who want to get me
are mean and cunning and strong.
I need someone brave to help me:
O God, send someone along.

The bullies who want to get me
are waiting to hurt and jeer.
I need someone kind to help me:
O God, send somebody near.

The bullies who want to get me
are ruining every day.
I need someone here to help me
and just make them go away.

256 Alone in the Playground

Dear God,
Knowing you are with me when I'm alone
in the playground doesn't really solve the
problem. It still looks as if I have no friends.

Dear God,
Help me find some friends.

257 Prayer of a Bully

Dear God,
I don't mean to be mean.
I would like to be liked.
It would help if you helped.

258 Give Me Courage to Be Kind

Dear God,
It's so hard to go against the in-crowd and
be kind to someone everybody hates. Give
me courage and help me to imagine what
that person must be feeling.

Victoria Tebbs

259 Whispering in My Head

O God,
Close my ears to the whispering and the
sniggering and the name-calling of those
who want to torment me.

I hear them in the playground, I hear
them in the corridor, I hear them on the
way home.

Worst of all, I hear them in my head when
I am alone in my room and when I am
awake in the night.

O God,
Close my ears to ignore them, and open my
mouth to tell on them, not because I am
mean, but because I am brave to stop their
nastiness spreading even further.

260 No Revenge

Dear God,
When someone does me wrong, may I not
seek revenge.

ENDINGS AND BEGINNINGS

261 Thank You for All Days

Thank you for schooldays.
Thank you for holidays.
Thank you for all days.
Thank you, God, always.

262 Moving On

A time to remember the good days.
A time to remember the bad days.
A time to cling on.
A time to move forward.
A time to say goodbye and thank you.

Victoria Tebbs

263 Goodbye, Dear Old School

Goodbye, dear old school,
Hello, bright new start.
May God guide our lives,
Head and hand and heart.

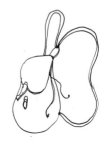

7 Things We Do

264 God-given Talents

Help us, dear God, to believe that our talents
are specially given by you.
Make us both careful and also courageous
in all of the things that we do.

265 Carry On Trying

When I feel I'm not as clever or successful
at what I do as my friends, help me to carry
on trying.

Olwen Turchetta

266 Join In?

Thank you for the things we love.
Are you watching from above?
As we play and draw and sing,
do you wish you could join in?

Victoria Tebbs

ARTS AND CRAFTS

267 The Play

Now the house lights dim
And soon our show must start.
Now we ask that God
Will help us play our part.

268 Music

Dear God,
We are a band of musicians.
Help us to play together, whether it is
our turn to play the tune, to play the
harmony, or to keep silent.

269 Playing the Piano

May my hands learn to play the piano.
May my heart learn to play the piano.
May my soul learn to play the piano.

270 Praise God with Music

Let us praise God
who does wonderful things.

Praise him with cymbals,
Praise him with drums and tambourines,
Praise him with chime bars and maracas,
Praise him with violins and cellos,
Praise him with recorders,
Praise him with singing,
Praise him with loud and lovely singing.

Let us praise God
who does wonderful things.

Based on Psalm 150

271 The Spirit of God

The spirit of God sets the trees dancing.
The spirit of God sets the flowers dancing.
The spirit of God sets the waters dancing.
May the spirit of God set me dancing.

272 Being Creative with Materials

Dear God,
Teach us to respect the materials we work
with: the paper and the paint, the clay and
the fabric. May we not waste them nor spoil
them, but use our imagination to make the
most of their special qualities and to make
something that is original and lovely.

273 Craftwork

Dear God,
Inspire our craftwork. Help us to make
things that are simple, strong and fit for
their purpose.

274 Practice

Dear God,
Bless this practice time.
May I get better at doing things right,
Not faster at doing things wrong.

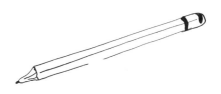

275 A Hard Job

This job is as hard as a mountain,
This job is as big as the sky.
O God, show me how to begin it
Or else, I'm afraid, I will cry.

Sports

276 Teams

Help us to work as a team.
– May we respect one another for our
different talents.

Help us to work as a team.
– May we enable one another to do the best
we can.

Help us to work as a team.
– May we care for one another in good times
and in bad times.

277 Team Games

Dear God,
I'm not good at team games.
But sometimes,
just sometimes,
may I get picked for the strong team
so I have have a bit of the fun
of winning.

Dear God,
I'm quite good at team games.
But often,
too often,
I get dumped in the weak team.
Help me to learn something
from losing.

278 Sports Day

Dear God,
If I win
help me not to gloat.
If I lose
help me not to cry.

279 Only a Game

"Don't get upset,"
they told me.
"It's only a game."

ONLY A GAME!

Dear God,
How can anything
be only a game?
The time it takes to play
is still part of real life.

280 Winning and Losing

Dear God,
Let us remember that this sport is about
playing to win and learning to lose.

281 Ball Game

Dear God,
Help us all to play well
and remind us that this is a game
for the building of friendships,
not a war for the destruction of enemies.

OUTDOOR ADVENTURES

282 A Great Adventure

We stand on the edge of a great adventure.

It will test our strength.
It will test our courage.
It will test our friendship.

May we find new strength.
May we find new courage.
May we find new friendship.

May we return stronger,
bolder,
kinder,
wiser.

283 Learning to Swim

As I learn to swim,
keep my legs from sinking.

As I learn to swim,
keep my head from sinking.

As I learn to swim,
keep my heart from sinking.

As I learn to swim,
keep my spirits from sinking.

284 Cyclist's Prayer

God,
Please teach me how it feels
to stay balanced on two wheels.

285 Learning to Cycle

Bless those who are learning to cycle
on three wheels.
Bless those who are learning to cycle
on two wheels.
Bless those who are learning to cycle
on one wheel.

286 For a Walking Holiday

Bless our boots
and bless our socks
as we scramble over rocks;
bless our compass,
bless our path,
bring us safely home at last.

287 A Backpacker's Prayer

Dear God,
Help me to learn that I cannot carry
the world upon my shoulders.

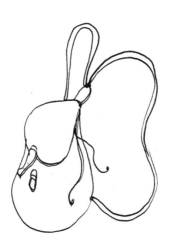

288 The Hiker's Rhyme

Up the hill and
Up the hill and
Up the hill I go:
Angels, come and push me please –
I'm getting really slow.

Up the hill and
Up the hill and
Up the hill I plod:
Angels, come and pull me please –
I'm feeling really odd.

Up the hill and
Up the hill and
Up the hill I climb:
Angels, come and join with me
to say the hiker's rhyme.

289 The Canoeist's Prayer

O God,
Let me not drift down the river of life,
but let me paddle it bravely
navigating the rocks and the rapids
and resting in quiet eddies.

290 The Nervous Abseiler

God of knot and God of rope,
Everything's in place (I hope)
As I creep along the ledge
Ready to jump off the edge.
May I hide the way I feel –
Give me courage not to squeal.
God of every rope and knot,
Is this fun? Hmm: not a lot.

291 Camping Prayer

Dear God,
From wind and rain
Protect us.

From cold and damp
Protect us.

From mud and sand
Protect us.

For camping fun
Prepare us!

292 My Tent

Guard this tent
Through wind and rain
Bring us safely
Home again.

Victoria Tebbs

HOLIDAYS

293 Busy Holidays

Holidays should be busy times
To fill with loads of fun;
To laugh and sing, to scream and shout,
To skip and jump and run.

O God, wake up the Aging Ones
Who say they need a rest;
Remind them WE'RE ON HOLIDAY
And busy days are best.

294 Holiday at Home

An hour is as long as a million years
– there's nothing to do but play!
Dear God, make me cheerful, helpful
    and kind
through all of this at-home day.

295 Travel Light

Dear God,
May I have all I need
And no more
So I can travel light:
Light of load
And light of heart.

296 Long Summer Holidays

Thank you, dear God,
for summer days
and summer adventures
and summer holidays so long
it seems that life will go on for ever.

297 Sand Between My Toes

I love to have sand between my toes,
to watch the tide as it comes and goes,
to pick up shells and throw them away:
thank you, dear God, for my holiday.

298 For a Seaside Holiday

O God, you have counted each grain of
  the sand
and the shells that lie washed on the shore.
Please keep us all safe, as if holding your hand
through this day, through this week, evermore.

8 Journeys

299 Walking Alone

Walking alone,
just me and God;
alone, just God and me.

Walking along
and trusting God
knows where I want to be.

300 Walking

Walking walking walking
An angel at my side;
Walking walking walking
An angel for my guide.
Walking walking walking
A journey without end;
Walking walking walking
An angel for my friend.

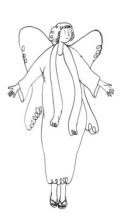

301 Fast or Slow

My journey may be fast or
My journey may be slow;
May God be always with me
Wherever I may go.

COURAGE AND PATIENCE ON JOURNEYS

302 Walking Gently

Dear God,
May we walk gently through this
fragile world.

303 New Paths

Dear God,
Make me brave to explore new paths.

304 Crossing the Street

May angels help me
when I cross the street:
keeping me watchful,
directing my feet.

305 The Family Car

There's air in the tyres
And fuel in the tank:
For this dear old car,
O God, we give thanks.

We're strapped in our seats,
The road is all clear.
We're off on our way
With God always near.

306 A Complicated Journey

Dear God,
We have a complicated journey ahead.
We want all its parts to join up into
    one smooth journey.
We want to arrive safely, with all our
    belongings.

We ask you to make things go well for us,
and to give us courage to deal with any
problems.

307 Waiting on a Journey

Though the time goes very slowly,
Help us, Lord, to make it holy;
Give us fresh imagination
To enjoy this recreation.

308 In a Traffic Jam

O God, we wish we were nearly there,
but sadly we're only here;
so give us patience to wait in calm,
an hour, a week or a year.

309 Waiting at the Airport

O God, this wait at the airport
Is getting too long for me;
It's not my idea of heaven –
It's just an eternity.

310 Scared of Flying

Dear God, I am like a baby bird:
too scared to fly.
Dear God, bless the air that holds the plane
up in the sky.

311 Taking to the Air

God of the albatross and the eagle,
the seagull and the swan:
you made their wings
and gave them the air to fly in.

God of the kiwi and the ostrich,
give courage to those who have no wings to fly
when they take to the air in planes.

312 Travelling Bravely

May I travel bravely
and arrive quite safely.

313 Outward and Homeward

Please give me courage for the
    outward journey;
please give me joy for the
    homeward journey.

Help Us Find Our Way

314 Lead Us Through this Day

Father, lead us through this day
As we travel on our way.
Be our safety, be our friend,
Bring us to our journey's end.

315 Protect Us in this Boat

God protect us
in this boat;
may it always
stay afloat.

316 Tiny Boat, Big Sea

A tiny boat
a great big sea
a guardian angel
watching me.

317 Look Upon My Boat and Me

Dear God, look from your heaven
Upon my boat and me;
Protect me from the billows
Of the great and stormy sea.

318 We Are Not Completely Lost

Dear God,
We have lost our way.
But we have not lost ourselves,
We have not lost our faith,
We have not lost our hope,
And we have not lost our love
 for one another.
Dear God,
Help us find our way.

319 Lead Kindly Light

Lead kindly light, amid the encircling
  gloom,
Lead thou me on;
The night is dark, and I am far from home;
Lead thou me on.
Keep thou my feet; I do not ask to see
The distant scene; one step enough for me.

John Henry Newman (1801–90)

320 Lost and Alone

I have lost my way
and I am beginning to worry.

But I am still alive
under God's heaven,
and God has given me a brain
to make a plan
that will get me home safely.

Dear God,
Help me make a good plan.

321 **Alone with God**

Alone with none but thee, my God,
I journey on my way.
What need I fear, when thou art near
O king of night and day?
More safe am I within thy hand
Than if a host did round me stand.

St Columba (521–97)

SEARCHING FOR GOD

322 **On a Journey**

I am a pilgrim
on a journey
to the place
where God is found;
every step
along that journey
is upon
God's holy ground.

323 Journey to Heaven

The here and now is flying by,
drifting, swirling, whirling by;
take me, lift me, let me fly
through my days to heaven on high.

324 St Patrick's Breastplate

May the strength of God pilot us.
May the power of God preserve us.
May the wisdom of God instruct us.
May the hand of God protect us.
May the way of God direct us.
May the shield of God defend us.
May the host of God guard us against
the snares of evil and the temptations
of the world.

St Patrick (389–461)

325 New Experiences

Dear God,
This journey is about visiting new places.

This journey is about enjoying new
adventures.

This journey is about making new
friendships.

This journey is about discovering new
wisdom.

Dear God,
May our journey be successful.

326 Discovering Ourselves and God

Dear God,
As we discover the world,
may we discover our true selves
and your unfailing love.

PARTINGS AND BLESSINGS

327 God Be with You

Wherever you go,
May God the Father be with you.
Wherever you go,
May God the Son be with you.
Wherever you go,
May God the Spirit be with you.

328 May the Road Rise to Meet You

May the road rise to meet you.
May the wind be always at your back.
May the sun shine warm upon your face,
the rains fall soft upon your fields and,
until we meet again,
may God hold you in the palm of his hand.

Irish blessing

329 A Parting of the Ways

We stand at a parting of the ways.
We thank God for the companionship
   we have enjoyed,
for the things we have done together
and the things we have learned together.

We ask God to bless us as we go our
   separate ways,
knowing that there will be uphills and
   downhills,
good times and bad times.

We pray that we will find new friendships
   and new challenges.
We pray that God will give us faith and
   hope at all times,
and surround us with unfailing love.

330 May the Lord Bless You

May the Lord bless you,
may the Lord take care of you;
May the Lord be kind to you,
may the Lord be gracious to you;
May the Lord look on you with favour,
may the Lord give you peace.

From Numbers 6:24–26

9 Health

331 My Body

Dear God,
Thank you for my body,
for it holds my life together.

May I live my life well inside it
so I may live long in this world
and for ever in heaven.

332 Thank You for My Body

Thank you, God,
for eyes and seeing;
for ears and hearing;
for a nose and smelling;
for a tongue and tasting;
for skin and feeling;
thank you for my body:
my passport to the world.

333 My Body is Precious

My body is precious: God made it for me.
May I take good care of it.

Victoria Tebbs

USING MY BODY WELL

334 Good at Sport

Dear God,
Help me to find a sport that my body
is good at.

335 Being Active

Thank you, God, that I can walk and run
  on the earth.
Thank you, God, that I can dive and swim
  in the water.
Thank you, God, that I can leap and fall
  through the air.
Thank you, God, that I can do everything
  under the sun.

336 Doing What is Needed

Dear God,
May my feet be ready to go to where
    I am needed.
May my hands be ready to do the things
    that are needed.
May my ears be ready to listen to what
    is needed.
May my tongue be ready to say the things
    that are needed.

337 Serving God

Some people serve God with their strength.
Some people serve God with their weakness.
Some people serve God with their
    cleverness.
Some people serve God with their
    simplicity.
May all people serve God with their all.

CARING FOR MY BODY

338 Going to the Dentist

Bless all dentists, give them skill
should they need to poke and drill;
and, if needs be, by your grace,
help me to endure a brace.

339 Bless My Teeth

Bless my teeth, O Lord, I pray,
For I brush them night and day;
Keep them safe, Lord, I implore,
In my mouth for evermore.

340 Glasses

Dear God,
Thank you for glasses:
glasses for eyes that need help;
glasses for eyes that need shade;
glasses to remind us
that not everyone sees the world
    the same way
with or without glasses.

341 Prayer for Knees

Some people fall to their knees in prayer
But I simply fall on my knees
Because I have rather tangly feet
O God, will you heal me, please?

342 Waiting Patiently

In the doctor's waiting room
here we sit and wait
for about a thousand years
'cos the doctor's late.

ILLNESS

343 Feeling Poorly

Feeling poorly in my bed
Feeling poorly in my head,
Feeling poorly, feeling pain:
God, please make me well again.

344 Winter Sniffles

A prayer for winter sniffles
A prayer for winter sneezes
A prayer said in a croaky voice
With little grunts and wheezes.

345 In My Bed

In my bed
and feeling rotten,
bored and gloomy
and forgotten.
May the angels
in the sky
watch to check
I do not die.
May the angels
here on land
come and hold me
by the hand.

346 Fractures

Dear God, I believe you can heal fractures.
I feel it in my bones.

347 After an Accident

Day by day, dear Lord, may my body heal.
Day by day, dear Lord, may my strength
    return.
Day by day, dear Lord, may my memories
    heal.
Day by day, dear Lord, may my smile
    return.

348 Hospital

I'm feeling alone in hospital,
And nobody seems to care.
Remember, God, I want to go home,
So hurry with that repair.

349 Sickbed Blessing

The blessing of clean bedclothes
The blessing of soft pillows
The blessing of cool water
The blessing of quiet sleep.

350 Sickness

Dear God, let me sleep the aching away.
Dear God, let me sleep the weakness away.
Dear God, let me sleep the tiredness away.
Dear God, let me sleep the long hours away.

351 Letting Go

Dear God,
Sometimes I feel so ill I am afraid I will
let go of life.
Dear God,
Never let go of me.

THINGS WE CAN AND CAN'T DO

352 Descriptions

I said to the person who could not see,
"Daffodils are the colour of warm sunshine
after cool rain."

I said to the person who could not hear,
"Birdsong looks like a firework of flowers."

And then I said to God,
"Talk to me about heaven, because
I cannot see it. And tell me what the
angels sing, for I have never heard them."

"Come and sit with me in the spring
morning," replied God, "and I will try
to explain."

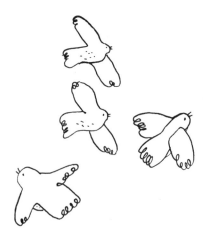

353 Playing Our Part

There are activities in which we can
    take part.
There are activities when we have
    to sit on the sidelines.
Help us to play all our parts well,
    and to cheer from the sidelines.

354 Using Our Talents

Dear God,
Please help each and every one of us to find
out what we're good at, and help us to use
our talents to help one another.

355 Giving and Receiving Love

Dear God,
I was not born strong.
I can only do a few things.
But I can give love
and I can receive love.

For this I give thanks.

356 Following Jesus

Lord Jesus,
Work your miracles among us.

May those who are blind see your face;
may those who are deaf hear your voice;
may those who cannot walk learn to
follow you.

Amen

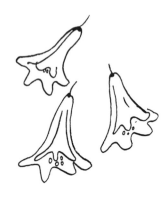

10 Sad Times

357 You Are My Light

Lord Jesus, you are my light
In the darkness,
You are my warmth
In the cold,
You are my happiness
In sorrow…

Anonymous

358 Make Me an Instrument of Your Peace

Lord, make me an instrument of your peace.
Where there is hatred, let me sow love;
Where there is injury, pardon;
Where there is discord, union;
Where there is doubt, faith;
Where there is despair, hope;
Where there is darkness, light;
Where there is sadness, joy.

O divine Master, grant that I may not so
much seek to be consoled as to console, to be
understood as to understand, to be loved as
to love; for it is in giving that we receive, it is
in pardoning that we are pardoned, and it is
in dying that we are born to eternal life.

Attributed to St Francis of Assisi (1181–1226)

Everyday Sadness

359 In the Light of Eternity

Dear God,
The awful things that happened today
probably don't matter much in the light
of eternity, but that light isn't shining
very brightly.

360 Expecting Miracles

Dear God,
I want you to make things better,
and I am expecting miracles.

361 The Broken Window

I broke a window
and I feel so ashamed.
People tried to cheer me up.
"It's not the end of the world,"
they said.

But it feels like the end. Dear God, help
me do what I can to get things mended,
and make me cheerful again.

362 Haunted by a Worry

Dear God,
I am haunted by a worry like a half-seen
shadow.

It stalks me in the daytime and it besieges
me in the night-time.

Dear God,
Command that worry to show itself clearly
in the light, and together let us send it away.

363 A Friend to the Lonely

O God,
Be near to those who are lonely;
Comfort those who despair;

Make me a friend to the lonely
And a helper to those in need.

364 Deeply Gloomy

Deeply gloomy
Deeply sad
When the day
Goes deeply bad.

Deeply hoping
God above
Will enfold me
In his love.

365 Today is Difficult

We pray for those for whom today
is like the windswept mountain:
give them comfort.

We pray for those for whom today
is like the stormy sea:
give them calm.

We pray for those for whom today
is like the darkest night:
give them hope.

Sophie Piper

366 Morning Faces and Morning Hearts

When the day returns call us up with
morning faces, and with morning hearts,
eager to labour, happy if happiness be our
portion, and if the day is marked for sorrow,
strong to endure.

Robert Louis Stevenson (1850–94)
(Written and read to his family by R.L. Stevenson
the day before he died)

367 Tough Times

Yesterday was difficult. Today was hard.
Tomorrow will be tough. In this time of
trouble, keep close to me, God, and remind
me of your everlasting comfort for those
in need.

Victoria Tebbs

368 Fill Us with Your Love

Lord Jesus Christ...
fill us with your love
that we may count nothing too small
   to do for you,
nothing too much to give,
and nothing too hard to bear.

St Ignatius Loyola (1491–1556)

369 Love is Giving

Love is giving, not taking,
mending, not breaking,
trusting, believing,
never deceiving,
patiently bearing
and faithfully sharing
each joy, every sorrow,
today and tomorrow.

Anonymous

Dark Times

370 Sorrow

Flood of sorrow, flood of tears
Like the flood of ancient years

Now in grief my world is drowned
Storm and cloud are all around

Pull me to the ark of love
Set your rainbow high above

Let my world grow new and green
Let the tree of peace be seen.

371 God Our Help

O God, our help in ages past,
our hope for years to come,
be thou our guard while troubles last,
and our eternal home.

Isaac Watts (1674–1748)

372 Whisper

A whispered prayer
For calm and peace
In a troubled place;

A whispered prayer
For quietness,
Gentleness and grace.

373 Nobody Knows the Trouble I See

Nobody knows the trouble I see,
  nobody knows but Jesus.
Nobody knows the trouble I see,
  Glory Hallelujah!

Sometimes I'm up, sometimes I'm down,
  Oh yes, Lord!
Sometimes I'm almost to the groun',
  Oh yes, Lord.

Although you see me going along,
  Oh yes, Lord!
I have troubles here below,
  Oh yes, Lord.

What makes old Satan hate me so,
  Oh yes, Lord!
'Cause he got me once and let me go,
  Oh yes, Lord.

Nobody knows the trouble I see,
  nobody knows but Jesus.
Nobody knows the trouble I see,
  Glory Hallelujah!

Black spiritual

374 Perhaps the Earth Will Crumble

O God,
I am uncertain.
I am afraid.
My imagination runs wild.
Perhaps the earth will crumble beneath me
and I will fall into endless darkness.

O God,
Keep my feet on holy ground
and shine the golden light of heaven on
   a safe path.

375 Thy Way, Not Mine

Thy way, not mine, O Lord,
However dark it be;
Lead me by thine own hand,
Choose out the path for me.

Horatio Bonar (1808–89)

376 Watch Over Us

Keep watch, dear Lord, with those who work,
or watch, or weep this night, and give your
angels charge over those who sleep.

Tend the sick, Lord Christ; give rest to the
weary, bless the dying, soothe the suffering,
pity the afflicted, shield the joyous; and all
for your love's sake.

St Augustine (354–430)

377 Your Kingdom Come

Heavenly Father,
may your kingdom come:
may those who have forgotten you
    remember your love;
may those who are trapped by wrongdoing
    believe in your forgiveness;
may those who have lost their way know
    your guiding;
and so may there be joy in heaven today.

Amen

Based on Matthew 6:9–13

378 Sorrow as Deep as the Ocean

Sorrow as deep as the ocean
Grief like a drowning wave
Faith like the frailest coracle
God alone strong to save.

379 Shining in Darkness

Jesus bids us shine
   With a pure, clear light,
Like a little candle
   Burning in the night;
In this world of darkness,
   So we must shine,
You in your small corner,
   And I in mine.

Anonymous

380 All Things Work Together

Dear God,
You can make all things work together
  for the good.
Take this moment of failure and
  disappointment
and make it part of my journey to wisdom
  and happiness.

381 With Us in Sorrow

God has not promised a world without
sorrow; but God has promised to be with
us in our sorrow.

382 An End to Sorrow

Come, O Joy:
Let heaven break into my dark night of
sorrow like the early dawn of a summer
morning.

Bible Words for Sad Times

383 I Have Been Crying in the Night

I have been crying in the night, O God;
my pillow is wet with tears.
I am too tired to face the day,
too scared to face those who hate me.

Keep me safe from those evil people;
listen to my cry for help.
Bring all their wickedness to an end;
answer my prayer.

From Psalm 6

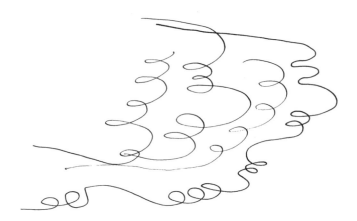

384 I Need Help!

My God, my God, why have you
   abandoned me?
I have cried desperately for help, but still
   it does not come.

It was you who brought me safely
   through birth,
   and when I was a baby, you kept me safe.
I have relied on you since the day I was born,
   and you have always been my God.
Do not stay away from me!
   Trouble is near, and there is no one to help.

O Lord, don't stay away from me!
   Come quickly to my rescue!

Psalm 22:1, 9–11, 19

385 The Lord is My Shepherd

The Lord is my shepherd;
  I have everything I need.
He lets me rest in fields of green grass
  and leads me to quiet pools of fresh water.
He gives me new strength.
He guides me in the right paths,
  as he has promised.
Even if I go through the deepest darkness,
  I will not be afraid, Lord,
    for you are with me.
Your shepherd's rod and staff protect me.

You prepare a banquet for me,
  where all my enemies can see me;
you welcome me as an honoured guest
  and fill my cup to the brim.
I know that your goodness and love will be
  with me all my life;
  and your house will be my home as long
    as I live.

Psalm 23

386 You Are My Shepherd

Dear God, you are my shepherd,
You give me all I need,
You take me where the grass grows green
And I can safely feed.

You take me where the water
Is quiet and cool and clear;
And there I rest and know I'm safe
For you are always near.

Based on Psalm 23

387 The Lord Protects Me from
All Danger

The Lord is my light and my salvation;
I will fear no one.
The Lord protects me from all danger;
I will never be afraid.

Psalm 27:1

388 Why Am I So Sad?

Why am I so sad?
  Why am I so troubled?
I will put my hope in God,
  and once again I will praise him,
  my saviour and my God.

Psalm 42:11 and 43:5

389 God is Our Shelter

God is our shelter and strength,
  always ready to help in times of trouble.
So we will not be afraid, even if the earth
    is shaken
  and mountains fall into the ocean depths;
even if the seas roar and rage,
  and the hills are shaken by the violence.

Psalm 46:1–3

390 In Trouble

In trouble, right up to my neck,
and sinking in slimiest mud;
in trouble, in trouble so deep,
surrounded by storm and by flood.

O God, hear me crying for help,
and don't let me sink to the grave;
because of your unfailing love,
may you, Lord, come swiftly to save.

From Psalm 69

391 At Peace

Lord, I have given up my pride
    and turned away from my arrogance.
I am not concerned with great matters
    or with subjects too difficult for me.
Instead, I am content and at peace.
As a child lies quietly in its mother's arms,
    so my heart is quiet within me.

Psalm 131:1–2

392 Do Not Abandon Me!

When I was a child,
God loved me,
God called me,
God taught me to walk,
God held me in his loving arms,
God fed me and gave me all I needed.

But I turned away
and now everything has gone wrong.

O God,
do not abandon me now!
Do not be angry,
for you are God,
the Holy One.

Based on Hosea 11:1–9

393 Shelter Me

O God,
be to me
like the evergreen tree
and shelter me in your shade,
and bless me again
like the warm gentle rain
that gives life to all you have made.

Based on Hosea 14:4–8

394 I Called and You Answered

In my distress, O Lord, I called to you.

Deep in the troubled waters, I called to you.

Wrapped in the slime of the sea, I called
  to you.

Down by the gates of the dead, I called
  to you.

In my distress, O Lord, I called to you,
and you answered me.

Based on Jonah's prayer, Jonah 2

395 Save Us!

Save us, Lord:
the storm is blowing us,
the sea is tossing us
and we are about to die.

Based on Matthew 8:25

396 In Our Troubles

Thank you, God, that you help us in our
troubles, so that we can help others who
have all kinds of troubles.

From 2 Corinthians 1:4

397 Give Me Peace

I will not worry,
dear God,
but I will ask you for the things I need
and give thanks.

Give me the peace that comes from knowing
that all my worries are safe with you.

From Philippians 4:6–7

11 Saying Goodbye

398 Life

Dear God,
I offer you my life
In its unfolding springtime:
Confident of its summer,
Curious about its autumn,
Careless of its winter.
Dear God,
I trust you with my life
And with my death.

399 Life's Pattern

Thank you, dear God, for marking out our
years with the pattern of the seasons: with
leaves unfolding, flowers blooming, seeds
falling, new life in the dark earth waiting.

400 The Beauty of Life and Death

O God,
May we learn from the seasons
the beauty of living
and the beauty of dying.

401 Sea of Everlasting Dreams

God bless the boat that is my life
and float me down the stream
of happy years, then to the sea
of everlasting dreams.

402 Living Well

Help me to live this day well,
from its beginning to its ending.

Help me to live my life well,
from its beginning to its ending.

403 You Are with Me

My Lord God, I have no idea where I am
going. I do not see the road ahead of me.
I cannot know for certain where it will
end… Therefore I will trust you always
though I may seem to be lost and in the
shadow of death. I will not fear for you are
ever with me, and you will never leave me
to face my perils alone.

Anonymous

404 Come Close By

I know that I
must one day die
and so I sigh:
Lord, come close by.

GRIEVING

405 Grief

Dear God,
Give us courage
in the night-time of our grief
to trust in your keeping
and the certainty of morning.

406 Missing

Dear God,
I am missing someone so badly.
There is a hole in my days,
in my evenings,
in my life.
Dear God,
How can I survive the pain
of missing?

407 Give Me Comfort

Death, like the bare winter's earth;
Tears, like the shivering rain;
Grief, like the dark winter's night;
God, give me springtime again.

408 Hold My Hand

As the rain hides the stars,
as the autumn mist hides the hills,
as the clouds veil the blue of the sky,
so the dark happenings of my lot
hide the shining of your face from me.
Yet, if I may hold your hand in the
darkness, it is enough. Since I know
that, though I may stumble in my
going, you do not fall.

Gaelic prayer (translated by Alistair MacLean)

409 The Path that Leads to the End

Dear God,
This is the path that leads to the end of
life. We do not know how far there is to
go, and the travelling makes us weary. Give
us strength to walk the way one step at a
time, and to look for little things to cheer
us. Take away our fear of the unknown,
and help us to know for sure that you are
with us.

410 Saying Goodbye

Dear God,
We turn to the sunset horizon
and say our sad goodbyes.

We turn to the sunrise horizon,
trusting in your tomorrow.

411 Lead Me Through the Darkness

Lead me through the darkness
where I cannot see my way;
make a path for me to walk
into the light of day.

412 Things to Say

O God,
We didn't have time
to say what we meant to say.

There were things to say sorry for,
things to say thank you for,
things to remember together one more time
before we said goodbye.

O God,
Whisper to us what they would have said.
Whisper to them what we would have said.

413 Regrets and Resolutions

O God,
The person I loved has died, and there were
so many more things I should have done for
them and said to them.

Please forgive me; please let me forgive
myself.

Please let me live my life more wisely and
more kindly.

FOR SPECIAL SITUATIONS

414 For a Baby Never Born

Goodbye, little baby
who never was born,
we love you, we miss you,
we're feeling forlorn.

We trust that the angels
have wrapped you with love
and carried you gently
to heaven above.

415 For a Child in the Family

Dear God,
A child has died.
A part of our family has died.
A part of me has died.

Come and sit with us
in our sadness
and take each and every one of us
to a place where we can live again.

416 For a Classmate

Dear God,
We remember the life of a classmate
    and friend.
We remember their face and the sound
    of their voice.
We remember times we spent together
    and the things they did and said.
We think of the things they were
    especially good at...
We remember the things about them
    that sometimes made us cross.
We remember that they belonged with us,
    and we shared a part of our lives together.
We ask you to heal the pain we feel at
    their death.
We pray that you will comfort their family
    and relatives.
We ask you to welcome them into your
    presence with love and kindness.

Amen

417 For a Parent

Dear God,
My parent has died.
There will be no more talking together, nor
crying together, nor holding hands together.
Now it is time for the angels to take my
parent's hands and lead them to heaven.
Now it is time for the angels to take
my hands and lead me through the
world of grieving.
May the angels lead us gently.

418 Untimely Death

Dear God,
This death came too soon.
This person was too young.
This is not how life should end.

We weep at the cruelty of it all.
We wonder why you have let it happen.

We put ourselves into your arms and weep.

419 For Parents Who Have Lost a Child

Dear God,
We pray for parents who weep for a child,
and for all the hopes they once cradled
in their arms.

Dear God,
Although they are grown up,
take them in your arms
and cradle them.

420 When a Grandparent is Bereaved

Dear God,
Please take care of Gran in a house dark
    with goodbye and sadness.
Open the windows of happy memories and,
    in time, new possibilities.

421 For Gran

O God,
My Gran is suddenly alone in the world
    and in need of your special love:
the love that reaches between death and life,
between earth and heaven,
between now and eternity.

422 In Your Hand

O God,
Life and death are in your hand.

We give thanks for those
who arrive at death calmly
with enough time
to say goodbye.

We pray for those
whose life is snatched away,
who leave this world
in sudden confusion.

Help us to believe
that the life and death
of each and every one
are in your hand.

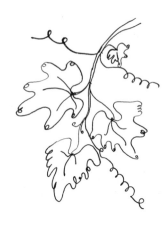

THE DEATH OF ANIMALS

423 An Animal on the Road

We weep, dear God,
at the blood that was spilt on the road.

We mourn, dear God,
for the body that was crushed on the road.

We pray, dear God,
for the life that was killed on the road.

May we learn, dear God,
to travel gently along the road.

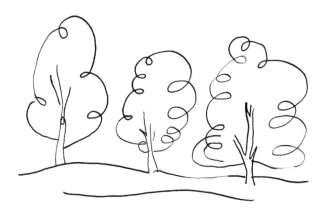

424 A Prayer for Little Tiny Things

A prayer for little tiny things
whose little life has flown:
may they be safe in God's great love –
they are God's very own.

425 For a Little Creature

Dear God,
Into your care we give this little creature
    who has died.
We lay a green leaf beside her, and
    remember her life.
We lay a brown leaf beside her, and mourn
    her death.
We scatter a handful of petals to the
    gentle wind
and trust that the life that has blown
    away from us
will be safe with you.

426 For My Cat

The basket where my cat slept
is empty, and the house is mournful
in its quiet stillness.
Dear God, thank you for my dear pet,
who brought me comfort
in moments of loneliness
and warmth on chilly winter days.

Victoria Tebbs

427 Goodbye to a Furry Friend

When little creatures die
And it's time to say goodbye
To a bright-eyed furry friend,
We know that God above
Will remember them with love:
A love that will never end.

REMEMBERING

428 We Remember

Every day
in silence we remember

those whom we loved
to whom we have said a last goodbye.

Every day
in silence we remember.

429 Laying Flowers

We lay flowers
and remember this person.

We lay flowers
and remember the sad times.

We lay flowers
and remember the glad times.

We lay flowers
and remember God's love.

430 A Funeral Wreath

An evergreen
for remembrance;
a faded leaf
for goodbye;
a pure white flower
for trust in God
and hope
of heaven on high.

431 We Give Them Back to You

We give them back to you dear Lord,
who gavest them to us.
Yet as thou didst not lose them in giving,
so we have not lost them by their return.
For what is thine is ours always, if we
are thine.

Quaker prayer

432 A Life Well Lived

Thank you, dear God, for this life well lived;
for the bright and sunny morning years,
and the long and busy daytime years;
for the quiet and lovely sunset years.

Now this life, like the setting sun,
has slipped beyond our horizon
and into your everlasting light.

433 Knowing More About Love

Dear God,
You lend us to this world
to love one another.

Now we must say goodbye
to someone we love
and who loved us.

At this time of parting,
may they know more of your love,
and may we know more of your love.

Amen

434 Protect My Heart

O God,
Protect my heart from the grief of goodbye.
Protect my heart from the grief of gone.

Walk with me to the quiet place
where I can look with calm upon eternity.

435 We Entrust Our Loved Ones to God

O God,
We ask you never to forget the one
we loved.

We entrust their body to the earth, with its
seasons of light and dark, rising and falling,
living and dying.

We entrust their soul to your heaven where
they may live for ever in the light of your
everlasting love.

436 Give Thanks

In the shadows of daytime
Give thanks for the sun.

In the shadows of night-time
Give thanks for the day.

In the shadows of sadness
Give thanks for all joy.

In the shadows of dying
Give thanks for all life.

HEREAFTER

437 Unbelieving

God bless those who died while unbelieving.
Welcome them, and comfort those left
grieving.

438 In Heaven's Streets

In heaven's streets
the cherry trees
are hung with blossoms white;
and you'll be there
for cherry time
if you would live aright.

439 Life Comes and Goes

Where does life come from?
God gives it.

Where does life go to?
God takes it.

440 Mending Broken Hearts

May kind earth take the body,
May heaven take the soul;
And though our hearts are broken,
May God soon make them whole.

441 Where Life Touches Death

We stand together
at the place where life touches death.

We stand together
at the place where light touches dark.

We stand together
at the place where earth touches heaven:

where, beyond death, is everlasting life;
where, beyond dark, is everlasting light.

442 The Parting of Ways

Goodbye
like an arctic winter:
cold, unending night.

Heaven
more than arctic summer:
everlasting light.

443 The End and the Beginning

To see you is the end and the beginning,
You carry us, and you go before.
You are the journey, and the journey's end.

Boethius (480–524)

444 A Place of Peace

Let dark earth
be a place of rest;
let bright heaven
be a place of peace.

445 Spinning in Mystery

Sometimes I think the earth is flat.

"No," you will say, "it is a round globe
spinning in space, and in that space are
stars and galaxies."

But no one has made the journey back
to the silver dawn that is before life began,
nor back from the golden sunset that is
after life has ended.

So I will reply that the world we live in is
spinning in mystery, and in that mystery,
I believe, is God and everlasting love.

446 Brightest Heaven

May death's grey door swing open
to reveal brightest heaven.

447 Trees of Heaven

Bless the autumn leaves that fall
and crumble in decay;
may the trees of heaven bloom
in everlasting day.

448 From Darkness to Light

The seed falls.
The winter is dark and cold.

The body of our loved one falls.
Our days are dark and cold.

The seed grows.
The spring is warm and bright.

You welcome our loved one to heaven.
May our days be warm and bright.

449 Life Goes On

Death will take the breath away
but God will take the soul;
though the body turn to ash
the life will be kept whole.

450 Life Has Left

The life has left
in one last sigh
and we must say
a fond goodbye.
Now may the God
of heaven above
receive the soul
with kindly love.

451 Room in Heaven

Kind Jesus,
Someone I love is dying. Make ready for them
their room in heaven.

Based on John 14:1–4

452 After Death

O God,
Give a reward to those who have been good –
Give them a safe journey through death
Give them joy that lasts for ever.

Based on part of a 13th-century hymn

453 Fit for Heaven

Someone I love has died. Their old body is no use to them any more. Dear God, raise them in a new body, beautiful and strong, and perfectly fit for heaven.

Based on 1 Corinthians 15

454 Lead Us to Heaven

O God,
Put an end to death.
Put an end to grief and crying and pain.
Make all things new.
Lead us to heaven.

From Revelation 21

455 Lead Us into Your Presence

O God,
You have not made us for darkness
but for light.

You have not made us for sorrow
but for joy.

You have not made us for death
but for life.

So lead us all into your presence.

456 Our End Which is No End

All shall be Amen and Alleluia.
We shall rest and we shall see.
We shall see and we shall know.
We shall know and we shall love.
We shall love and we shall praise.
Behold our end which is no end.

St Augustine (354–430)

12 Changing Seasons and Weather

457 Thank You for Our Senses

O God, we thank you for this earth, our home; for the wide sky and the blessed sun, for the salt sea and the running water, for the everlasting hills and the never-resting winds, for trees and the common grass underfoot.

We thank you for our senses by which we hear the songs of birds, and see the splendour of the summer fields, and taste of the autumn fruits, and rejoice in the feel of the snow, and smell the breath of the spring.

Grant us a heart wide open to all this beauty; and save our souls from being so blind that we pass unseeing when even the common thornbush is aflame with your glory, O God our creator, who lives and reigns for ever and ever.

Walter Rauschenbusch (1861–1918)

THE ELEMENTS

458 Fire, Water, Earth, Air

The fiery sun
tells of a glorious God.

The rolling sea
tells of a powerful God.

The deep brown earth
tells of a nurturing God.

The drifting air
tells of a gentle God.

459 Water

Thank you, God, for water:

cloud-breaking,
seed-waking,
soil-drenching,
thirst-quenching,
life-bringing,
praises-singing

water.

460 River

Let us learn how the rivers dance:

let us watch how they trickle and surge,
how they fall and curl,
how they swirl and eddy.

Let us see how they dance according to the
rules God gave them; how they are more
obedient to their Maker than any of
humankind.

Let us learn from the rivers how to dance
to the Maker's tune.

461 Earth

Dear God,
Thank you for the earth that holds us up,
and gravity that holds us down.

462 Sounds of Heaven

Sometimes
when I am down by the ocean
I imagine I can hear the waves
breaking on heaven's shore.

463 Praised Be My Lord and God

Praised be my Lord and God with all his
creatures, and especially our brother the
sun, who brings us the day, and who brings
us the light...

Praised be my Lord for our sister the moon,
and for the stars, which he has set clear and
lovely in heaven.

Praised be my Lord for our brother the wind,
and for air and cloud, calm and all weather...

Praised be my Lord for our sister water...

Praised be my Lord for our brother fire...

Praised be my Lord for our mother the earth,
which sustains us and brings forth different
fruits and flowers of many colours...

Praised be my Lord for all those who pardon
one another for his love's sake...

Praise ye and bless my Lord, and give him
thanks, and serve him with great humility.

Attributed to St Francis of Assisi (1182–1226)

464 Rock of Earth

Here on the ancient rock of earth
I sit and watch the sky;
I feel the breeze that moves the trees
While stately clouds float by.
I wonder why our planet home
Spins round and round the sun
And what will last for ever
When earth's days all are done.

465 Our Woodland Planet

Our little woodland planet
is alone among the stars
like a wild flower
on a bare mountain side,
with nothing to do
but marvel at the surrounding grandeur
and reflect the gentle beauty
of the One who made it all.

466 Where I Will See God's Face

I stand on the sand by the edge of the sea
and watch the waves roll by;
I look to the faraway misty line
where water touches sky;
I look at the shapes of the clouds in
   the blue
dissolving into space;
I dream of the heaven where God can be
   found,
where I will see God's face.

467 Grant Me Riches

Grant me riches
here on earth –
things that are
of priceless worth:

The shining sun
the silver sea
the diamond rain
the emerald tree.

For better far
than any gold
these treasures are
that none can hold.

468 Enjoy the World

Enjoy the world with your feet:
walk it.

Enjoy the world with your hands:
touch it.

Enjoy the world with your eyes:
admire it.

Enjoy the world with your nose:
smell it.

Enjoy the world with your ears:
listen to its music.

Enjoy the world with your whole body:
live in it.

469 May the Earth Be Kind

May the earth be kind to everyone:
pure cool water, flowing;
clean and clear air, blowing;
crops in good earth, growing;
golden sunshine, glowing.

470 Thy Glory Fills the Heaven

Lord, thy glory fills the heaven,
Earth is with its fullness stored;
Unto thee be glory given,
Holy, holy, holy Lord.

Bishop R. Mant (1776–1848)

471 God's Glory

The sunrise
tells of God's glory;
the moonrise
tells of God's glory;
the starshine
tells of God's glory;
the heavens
tell of God's glory.

Based on Psalm 19

472 Pied Beauty

Glory be to God for dappled things –
For skies of couple-colour as a brinded cow;
For rose-moles all in stipple upon trout that
    swim;
Fresh-firecoal chestnut-falls; finches' wings;
Landscape plotted and pieced – fold, fallow,
    and plough;
And all trades, their gear and tackle and trim.

All things counter, original, spare, strange;
Whatever is fickle, freckled (who knows how?)
With swift, slow; sweet, sour; adazzle, dim;
He fathers-forth whose beauty is past change:
    Praise him.

Gerard Manley Hopkins (1844–89)

473 Sky Colours

The morning clouds are orange and pink
As the sun climbs into the sky,
And white clouds drift in the faraway blue
At noon when the sun is high.
The sunset mixes up purple and mauve
With violet, gold and red,
And angels watch over me through the dark
When I'm asleep in my bed.

474 Choosing Colours

Dear God,
When I look at my paints and wonder
  which to choose,
May I be inspired by the ever-changing
  colours of the sky.

Victoria Tebbs

475 The Presence of God

Here in the wild country,
I am aware of the silence of the universe
and the emptiness beyond all imagining.

Then the breeze passes like a whisper,
a bird trills a brief carol
and the One Who Is comes to sit beside me
to watch the sunrise.

476 I Walk with Beauty

I walk with beauty before me.
I walk with beauty behind me.
I walk with beauty above me.
I walk with beauty around me.

Based on a Navajo night chant

477 The Cause of Nature

Nature is but a name for an effect,
Whose cause is God.

William Cowper (1731–1800)

478 The Infinite

I stand in the presence of the infinite beauty
   of the stars.
I stand in the presence of the infinite beauty
   of the moon.
I stand in the presence of the infinite beauty
   of the sky.
I stand in the presence of the infinite.

WEATHER

479 Stormy Weather

Let there be space for the flooding,
Let there be space for the storm,
Let there be space for the cosy place
Where we can be snug and warm.

480 Rain

God of Noah
God of flood
God of puddles
God of mud
God of rainbows
God of sky
Turn the weather
Round to dry.

481 Kisses of Rain

Thank you for the rain
that kisses my face
and makes me feel
alive again.

Victoria Tebbs

482 Grey and Green

Grey rain falling
Green world singing
All the world
Its praises bringing.

483 Low Clouds

Though the clouds are low
and raining,
keep our spirits high
and shining.

484 Thanks for the Sunshine

The sun is warm on my cheek
and it makes me glow inside.

Victoria Tebbs

485 Sunlit and Shady Places

We thank you, God, for sunlit places,
bright and warm.

We thank you, God, for shady places,
dim and cool.

486 Love in All Weather

The sun may shine
The rain may fall
God will always
Love us all.

Victoria Tebbs

487 Choose the Weather

On rainy days I pray for sun.
In burning heat I dream of snow.
I face the wind and wish for calm.
I love the sound when strong winds blow.

And so, dear God, my prayer is this:
choose weather that you think is right
for holidays and harvest-time;
for pleasant days and restful nights.

THE CIRCLE OF THE YEAR

488 Painting the Year

In winter, God takes a sheet of plain paper
and pencils in the outline of things.

In spring, God brings out a paintbox and
washes the background in blue and green
and yellow.

In summer, God adds bright details: pink
and red and orange and mauve.

In the autumn, God scatters golden glitter.

489 Spiral Stairway to Heaven

Summer and winter come round and round,
and through the years we climb the spiral
stairway to heaven.

490 The God of the Trees

I will remember the buds of spring
When summertime leaves are green;

I will remember their rippling shade
When colours of autumn are seen;

I will remember the red and the gold
When wintertime branches are bare;

I will give thanks to the God of the trees
Whose love reaches everywhere.

491 White Are the Wavetops

White are the wavetops,
White is the snow:
Great is the One
Who made all things below.

Green are the grasslands,
Green is the tree:
Great is the One
Who has made you and me.

Blue are the cornflowers,
Blue is the sky:
Great is the One
Who made all things on high.

Gold is the harvest,
Gold is the sun:
God is our Maker –
Great is the One.

492 Patterns of the Seasons

Thank you, God,
for the unchanging
patterns of the seasons:
the frosts of winter
melting into moist spring,
the rain-soaked buds

unfolding into bright summer,
the flowers fading and falling
in the autumn mist
leaving the year cold and bare,
lit by a pale sun
and the golden promise
of your unfailing love.

WINTER

493 Now the Wind is Coming

Now the wind is coming,
Now the wind is strong,
Now the winter freezes
And the darkness will be long.
Now we see the starlight
In the midnight sky,
We know God is with us
And the angels are close by.

494 Winter Storms

O thought I!
What a beautiful thing
God has made winter to be
by stripping the trees
and letting us see
their shapes and forms.
What a freedom does it seem
to give to the storms.

Dorothy Wordsworth (1771–1855)

495 Pure White Snow

I stand to gaze at the pure white snow
new from heaven on earth below.

496 Winter Wet

Dear God,
Thank you for the wild tangle of the
   woodlands
and the murky damp of ditch and bog.
Thank you for the sharp smell of crumble
   and decay
and for the winter wet in which old things
   pass away.

SPRING

497 Laughing Spring

I am laughing 'cos of spring,
Laughing 'cos of everything,
Laughing yellow, laughing blue,
Laughing 'cos of me and you,
Laughing blossom, laughing pink –
God is laughing too, I think.

498 Flames of Green

God has lit each wintry bough
with tiny flames of green,
and soon the woods are all ablaze
as springtime leaves are seen.

499 The Colour of Birdsong

Listen to the melody of green in the spring
morning;

and open your eyes to the colour of the
birdsong.

500 All is Well

All is well:
the leaves of grass are growing.
All is well:
the leaves of flowers are showing.
All is well:
the leaves of trees are blowing.
All is well:
God's springtime love is showing.

501 Greentime

The world has turned to greentime,
The trees are dressed in lace
And birds do sing
Of life and spring
And God's eternal grace.

SUMMER

502 Drifting Like a Seagull

Let me drift like a seagull
up in the summer sky
feeling the air grow golden
as the sun rises high.

Let me drift like a seagull
out on the sea so wide
feeling the ocean moving
as the moon pulls the tide.

Let me drift through the summer
down by the ocean shore
resting in God's creation
now and for evermore.

503 The Little Cares that Fretted Me

The little cares that fretted me,
I lost them yesterday
Among the fields above the sea,
Among the winds at play,
Among the lowing of the herds,
The rustling of the trees,
Among the singing of the birds,
The humming of the bees.

The foolish fears of what might pass
I cast them all away
Among the clover-scented grass,
Among the new-mown hay,
Among the hushing of the corn
Where drowsy poppies nod,
Where ill thoughts die and good are born –
Out in the fields with God.

Louise Imogen Guiney (1861–1920)

504 Thank You, God, for this Summer Day

Thank you, God, for this summer day;
Thank you, God, for this golden day;
Thank you, God, for this lazy day:
Thank you, God, for this holiday.

AUTUMN

505 Thanks for the Autumn

The golden leaves have turned to rust,
the silver clouds to grey;
we give thanks for the autumn
as the summer slips away.

506 Leaves of Autumn

Bless the leaves of autumn
as they fade and blow away;
summer may be over
but the memories will stay.

507 The Autumn Has Come

Dear God,
The autumn has come.
Time to look back with thanks.
Time to look forward with courage.

508 The Riches of Autumn

We thank you, Lord,
for all the riches of autumn:
bronze leaves,
silver spider's webs,
golden harvest.

509 Autumn Berries

Autumn berries
round and red:
by God's hand
the birds are fed.

Harvest

510 We Plough the Land

We plough the land,
God sends the rain
to bring the harvest
once again;
and when the fields
of wheat turn gold,
then God's great goodness
must be told.

Based on Psalm 65

511 Harvest

We harvest the fields,
we harvest the trees,
we harvest the gardens,
we harvest the seas.

We gather the blessings
that God freely gives
to you and to me
and to each one who lives.

512 We Plough the Fields, and Scatter

We plough the fields, and scatter
The good seed on the land.
But it is fed and watered by God's almighty
  hand.
He sends the snow in winter,
The warmth to swell the grain,
The breezes and the sunshine,
And soft refreshing rain:
All good gifts around us are sent from
  heaven above;
Then thank the Lord, O thank the Lord,
For all his love.

Matthias Claudius (1740–1815)

513 Plenty of Food

The harvests have ripened in the sun;
There's plenty of food for everyone:
There's some for ourselves and more
  to share
With all of God's people everywhere.

514 Autumnal Glories

For all the rich autumnal glories spread –
The flaming pageant of the ripening woods,
The fiery gorse, the heather-purpled hills;
The rustling leaves that fly before the wind
And lie below the hedgerows whispering;
For meadows silver-white with hoary dew;
The first crisp breath of wonder in the air,
We thank you, Lord.

Anonymous

515 Silver and Gold

Let there be silver rain.
Let there be golden grain.

516 Harvest-Sharing

Thank you, God, for all we have:
Enough, and more to share.
We bring these gifts for others now
To show them that we care.

517 Harvest-Home

Come, ye thankful people, come,
Raise the song of harvest-home!
All is safely gathered in,
Ere the winter storms begin;
God, our Maker, doth provide
For our wants to be supplied;
Come to God's own temple, come;
Raise the song of harvest-home!

G.J. Elvey (1816–93)

518 Harvest Gifts

Thank you, dear God, for our harvest
  garden.
Thank you for the seeds and the soil,
for the sun and the rain,
for the roots and the leaves and the ripening
  fruits.
As you have blessed us with harvest gifts,
  dear God,
may we bless others by sharing them.

519 For All the Harvests

For all the harvests of the world:
we give you thanks, O God.
For those who work to gather the crops:
we give you thanks, O God.
For those who fill our shops with food:
we give you thanks, O God.
For food to eat and food to share:
we give you thanks, O God.

520 Johnny Appleseed Grace

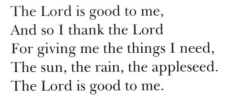

The Lord is good to me,
And so I thank the Lord
For giving me the things I need,
The sun, the rain, the appleseed.
The Lord is good to me.

*Attributed to John Chapman, American pioneer
and planter of orchards (1774–1845)*

521 The Harvest of Our Garden

The harvest of our garden
is astonishingly small;
but oh, dear God, we thank you
that there's anything at all.

522 Enjoying the Harvest

May the rain fall from heaven
and wash away the footprints of the wicked.

May the sun shine
and the crops ripen

and may ordinary people of good faith
enjoy the harvest.

523 A Rewarding Harvest

I take the seed, I go to sow
In name of Him who makes it grow.
I breathe the wind that blows so soft
And throw a handful high aloft.
Where the rock is hard and bare
No plant will sprout, no flower be there.
Where the seed falls to the soil
A harvest will reward my toil.

524 Harvest for All

Harvest of leaf,
Harvest of fruit,
Harvest of stem,
Harvest of root;
Harvest of lowland,
Harvest of hill,
Harvest that all
May eat their fill.

PLANTS

525 Bless the Seed

Dear God, bless the seed that we sow today
and let it grow into a tree;
and when we are old may we sit in its shade
and dream of eternity.

526 Plants in Dangerous Places

Thank you, great Maker God, for plants that
live in dangerous places, clinging to cliffs and
crags and crumbling walls. Thank you for
their unexpected beauty.

527 This Season's Collection

The Creator God,
fashion designer to the flowers,
is bringing out
this season's collection.

528 Prayer of the Seedling

I open my hands
to God's golden sunshine.

I fold my hands
in God's silver light.

I reach up tall
to touch God's blue heaven.

I trust in God
to grow up aright.

529 Pattern of Leaves

God has written the name of every tree
in the pattern of the bark.

Every tree writes its prayer to God
in the pattern of leaves against the sky.

530 I Hear God Speaking

Looking at the sky
while a tall tree sways
I hear God speaking
in a thousand different ways:
of melodies and miracles
that all are born on earth;
of dreams and possibilities
of everlasting worth.

531 A World to Share

I plant this tree for the earth.
I plant this tree for the air.
I plant this tree for the whole wide world
that God gave us all to share.

532 The Kingdom of God

The kingdom of God
is like a tree
growing through all eternity.

In its branches, birds may nest;
in its shade we all may rest.

533 God the Gardener

God is a fierce gardener:
clearing the overgrown world with fire
and flood, with windstorm and landslide.

God is a gentle gardener:
planting the bare earth with trailing
tendrils and tiny flowers.

God is all powerful; God is all love.

534 A Woodland Cathedral

The woods are God's own cathedral
with pillars that reach to the sky
and a faraway ceiling of fluttering leaves
where songbirds and angels fly.

535 The Light of God

As flowers turn to face the sun,
I turn my life to the light of faith,
the light of hope,
the light of love,
the light of God.

536 The Careful Creator

Who would make a tiny flower
so beautiful? It lasts an hour!
The bloom then quickly fades away
before the setting of the day.

Who would make a tiny leaf
so intricate? Its life is brief:
a season in the summer sun
before its fluttering life is done.

The One who made both great and small,
who loves and cares for one and all
on land and water, sky and sea:
the One who loves and cares for me.

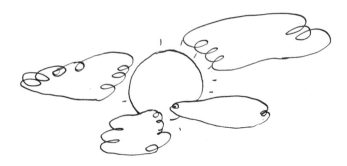

537 Tree Song

The trees grow down,
down into the earth,
right down into long ago.

The trees grow up,
up into the sky,
right up where the strong winds blow.

The trees, they sway,
they sway in the wind
and whisper a secret song:

"We thank you, God,
for keeping us safe,
that we might grow tall and strong."

538 For Wild Flowers

Dear God,
We give you thanks for the beautiful
plants you deliver to our garden from
the fields and the woodlands.

539 Showers and Flowers

For sun
and for showers,
for seeds
and for flowers,
we give you thanks,
O God.

13 Creatures Great and Small

540 All Things Bright and Beautiful

All things bright and beautiful,
All creatures great and small,
All things wise and wonderful,
The Lord God made them all.

Cecil Frances Alexander (1818–95)

ANIMALS AROUND US

541 About a Pet Dog

Dear God,
May I help my dog
to grow in dogginess.
May my dog help me
to grow in humanity.

542 Comfort from a Cat

Dear God,
Thank you for my cat.
Stroking him and hearing him
purr always makes me happier
when I'm feeling stressed or sad.

Olwen Turchetta

543 Keep My Gerbil Safe

Dear God,
I love my gerbil, with his bright eyes,
twitching whiskers and glossy coat.
Please keep him safe as he scampers
about his home and snoozes in his bed
of straw, and help me to feed and care
for him every day.

Jenni Dutton

544 Bless My Goldfish

Dear God,
Bless my goldfish.
Please keep him safe from harm, lonely
in his tank. Please help me remember to
feed him every day and keep his water
clean so his scales never lose their
bright orange gleam.

Caroline Knight

545 Diversity

Multicoloured animals
With stripes and dots and patches:
God made each one different –
There isn't one that matches.

546 Animals on the Road

God of rabbits,
God of toads,
Help all creatures
Cross the roads.

547 Wild Birds

The wild birds are calling out
their wild morning song
to praise the Maker God
to whom wild things belong.

548 What Has Happened to God's Creation?

Yesterday, I went out in the dawning.
I went down to the riverside
and in the golden light unfolding
I caught a glimpse of unspoilt heaven
and was about to praise the Creator God.

Then I heard the wild shrieking of the
    waterbirds.
They were fighting with furious flapping
    wings:
fighting for territory,
fighting for a mate,
fighting for food,
fighting to protect their young.

And then the sun shone its fierce hard glare
upon a world that I saw was spoilt,
riven with violence and fear and pain.

So I called out to the Creator God in
    bewilderment:
"Why is the world like this?
What has happened to your creation?
When will you make it new?"

549 The Music of God's Creatures

Have you heard the choir of all God's
   creatures –
the operatic whale
and the slightly off-key buffalo;
the timid, squeaky-voiced mouse
and the clear carolling of the blackbird?

Listen carefully:
listen for the high notes and the low notes,
for the solo and the chorus,
for the melody and the rhythm,
for the songs of love and the songs of war.

Listen for the song of all creation
in praise of the creator.

550 **Praise the Lord**

Praise the Lord
all blackbirds
and all people who sing tunefully.

Praise the Lord
all buffalo
and all people who bellow loudly.

Praise the Lord
all frogs
and all people who croak oddly.

551 **Butterfly Prayer**

I think the butterfly
says her prayer
by simply fluttering
in the air.

I think the prayer
of the butterfly
just dances up
to God on high.

552 God Made Us All

He prayeth best, who loveth best
All things both great and small;
For the dear God who loveth us,
He made and loveth all.

S.T. Coleridge (1772–1834)

553 Little Creatures

The little bugs that scurry,
The little beasts that creep
Among the grasses and the weeds
And where the leaves are deep:
All of them were made by God
As part of God's design.
Remember that the world is theirs,
Not only yours and mine.

554 A Safe Place for Animals

Bless our little garden. May it be a safe
place for all the little creatures that creep
and scurry through the grasses. May it
be a busy place for all the little creatures
that sip and nibble and munch among
the flowers. May it be a joyful place for
all the birds that sing in the trees.

555 Wild and Strange

Thank you, God, for birds that sing
from high up in the trees;
thank you for the butterflies
that dance upon the breeze.
Thank you for the wild beasts
of every stripe and hue.
Thank you for the whole round globe
of green and gold and blue.

Thank you, God, for lobsters
and the strange things of the sea.
Thank you for the insects –
the mosquito and the flea.
Thank you for the frogs and toads,
and bright-eyed things that lurk
among the ooze and mud and slime
and long-neglected murk.

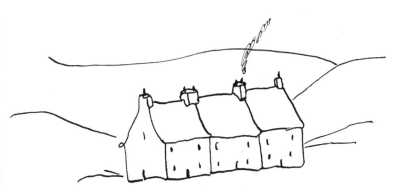

556 God Bless the Field and Bless the Furrow

God bless the field and bless the furrow,
Stream and branch and rabbit burrow...
Bless the minnow, bless the whale,
Bless the rainbow and the hail,
Bless the nest and bless the leaf,
Bless the righteous and the thief,
Bless the wing and bless the fin,
Bless the air I travel in,
Bless the mill and bless the mouse,
Bless the miller's bricken house,
Bless the earth and bless the sea,
God bless you and God bless me.

Anonymous

557 Lord of the Ocean

Lord of the ocean,
Lord of the sea:
Let all the fish swim
Strong and free.

Lord of the wavetops,
Lord of the shore:
Keep them all safe
For evermore.

558 Prayer for Kindness to Animals

We pray, Lord, for the humble beasts who
with us bear the burden and heat of the day,
giving their lives for the well-being of their
countries; and for the wild creatures, whom
you have made wise, strong and beautiful;
we ask for them your great tenderness of
heart, for you have promised to save both
man and beast, and great is your loving-
kindness, O Saviour of the world.

Russian prayer

559 Heaven's Music

If you have heard
the sound of birdsong
in the morning air,
then you will know
that heaven's music
reaches everywhere.

560 God Bless the Birds

God bless the birds of springtime
that twitter in the trees
and flutter in the hedgerows
and soar upon the breeze.

God bless the birds of summer
that gather on the shore
and glide above the ocean
where breakers crash and roar.

God bless the birds of autumn
as they prepare to fly
and fill the damp and chilly air
with wild and haunting cry.

God bless the birds of winter
that hop across the snow
and peck the fallen seeds and fruits
of summer long ago.

561 Evening Song

All praise to God for the evening song of
the birds. Whether the day has been good
or bad, whether we feel loved or unloved,
the birds still carol their cheerful songs as
the twilight comes and fades.

Animal Prayers

562 Prayer of the Caterpillar

Great Maker of the leaves,
why have you put me in this world?
I feel myself growing tired
of crawling, of eating, of living in fear.

Let me sleep,
oh, let me sleep long and deep;
and then let me awaken
to a bright new world
where I can dance.

563 Prayer of the Goldfish

Dear God,
The world I know
Is just a tiny globe
But beyond I glimpse
Amazing worlds
And I dream
Of an infinite ocean.

564 Prayer of the Spider

I spin for myself a web of prayer
that sways to and fro in the wafting air
as God walks by in the dawning light
when heaven is almost within our sight.

565 Prayer of the Ant

Dear God,
I belong to a big colony of ants.
I expect their prayers are the same as mine.
I expect my prayers are the same as theirs.
But I am wondering –
and I expect they are all wondering the
    same thing –
if you know each of us by a special name?

566 Prayer of the Shrew

Save me, dear God, from danger
that swoops down from the blue.
Hide me in a small safe place
and keep me close to you.

567 Prayer of the Hedgehog

Dear God,
Please be near to me.
No one else is.

568 Prayer of the Swallow

Dear God,
I was not made for winter.
Let me fly through the summerlands
to your heaven of everlasting light.

569 Prayer of the Skylark

I soar through the clear air
amazed at my own voice
and wondering if
there is an angel singing with me.

570 Prayer of the Wild Geese

O God,
Hear our cry.
The dark and cold are drawing near
and we are searching for a new homeland.
The way is long
and we grow weary
but will you,
O God,
please guide us.

571 Prayer of the Wolf

I am howling in the night, dear God;
howling alone,
howling aloud,
howling long, lonely howls
until I know that you have heard me.

572 Prayer of the Snake

No one can get any lower than me, O God,
and no one is more hated;
yet I have slithered into your presence
and you have not sent me away.

573 Prayer of the Chameleon

Dear God,
What strange creatures these humans are,
who judge one another by the colour of
their skin. Why, I and my kind, we change
the colour of our skin a dozen times, but
all the time we know that inside we are all
of equal worth.

574 Prayer of the Giraffe

Dear God,
Make my life outstanding.

575 **Prayer of the Lion**

Dear God,
I am weary of hunting.
I am tired of killing.
I want only to lie down
in the scorching afternoon heat
and dream of the time
when you will take your place
as king of the beasts
and everywhere is peace.

576 **Prayer of the Hippopotamus**

I thank you, God, that I am not like other
animals:

Not bone-thin, like the gazelle,
Not towering tall, like the giraffe,
Not noisy, like the gibbering monkeys.

I am glad that you have made me squat and
round and heavy so I can float at ease in the
cool water and wallow in the oozing mud.

Yet, for all that, I am not always perfect.

God have mercy on me, a hippopotamus.

577 Prayer of the Shark

Dear God,
I feel at home in the seas you have made.
I live my life the way you made me.
But I am afraid that other creatures hate me.
Dear God,
If there is a place for me in heaven,
may I not feel like a fish out of water there.

578 Prayer of the Whale

O God,
May the people of the world hear my song.
May it echo over the rolling sea,
and tell them of your greatness and your
   power,
and of love that reaches to the darkest deep.

579 Prayer of the Sloth

Dear God,
Give me a moment to think of what to say.

580 Prayer of the Owl

Now the night is over
Day is drawing near
Shade me from the sunshine
Drive away all fear.

Save me from the dangers
Of the clear blue day
God, while I lie sleeping,
Ever with me stay.

14 Looking After Our World

581 The Summer Brook

The winter brook flows quick and green
with swirling eddies in between
its tiny falls of sparkling spray
that curl and ripple on their way.

The summer brook is slow and grey
and choked with all we've thrown away:
old cans and bags and battered shoes
and things that we no longer use.

God our Maker, send the rain
to wash the whole world clean again
then teach us to respect and care
for water, fire, earth and air.

582 How to See the World

Dear God,
May we learn to see the world as other
people see it, and to appreciate their point
of view.

May we learn to see the world as you see it.

ENVIRONMENT

583 Silver, Blue, Gold, Green

O God, heal the scarred earth –

with silver and raining,
with blue and blowing,
with gold and shining,
with green and growing.

584 Litter

God's world is full of litter
and what we plan to do
is go and pick it up to make
the whole world good as new.

585 Spring Clean

Let the wind blow all the clouds away
And show us God's sky of blue;
Let us now throw all our rubbish away
And make our world clean and new.

586 The Garden and the City

Dear God,
You planted the Garden of Eden.
May we treat the wild lands as sacred.

You built the Heavenly City.
May we know that we build our cities
on holy ground.

587 Mending the World

Where the earth is ripped and torn
weave a web of green,
and add a patch of flowers so
the mend cannot be seen.

588 A Fallen World

Our world is fallen
as if from heaven.

Our world is broken
so we shall mend it.

Our world is wounded
so we shall heal it.

Our world is the Lord's,
and God will bless it.

589 A Damaged Landscape

Bind the wounded earth, dear Lord,
in bandages of green
and heal the scars where storm and flood
and lightning fire have been.

590 Respect the Earth

We think the earth is ours.

We dig it, drill it, plough it, mine it, pave it,
bomb it.

Then, from within the heart of things, the
earth erupts, it shakes, it quakes, it shifts,
it drifts.

May we learn to respect the earth, for it
is shaped by forces greater than our own,
and we should live in awe of them.

591 The Foundations of the Earth

Dear God,
May we not grow too proud of our
    buildings:
our tall towers
and our deep tunnels
and our long bridges.

May we remember that they are laid
upon the foundations of the earth,
the earth you made.

592 For City Streets and Woodland Paths

Thank you, God, for city streets:
their straight lines,
their hard, smooth paving.

Thank you, God, for woodland paths:
their winding ways,
their soft carpet of leaves.

593 Oh! For a Glimpse of the Stars

We give thanks for streetlamps that shine
  on our path,
but oh! for a glimpse of the stars
that wheel their way through the heavens
  above
with Jupiter, Venus and Mars.

We give thanks for pavements without ruts
  or holes,
but oh! for the smell of the earth,
the feel of tussocks and tree-roots and mud,
the planet that gave us our birth.

594 Built in a Sacred Place

A city is a temple of the material world
With buildings of brick and concrete, steel
  and glass,
Interlinking highways, secret alleyways,
An underground network of pipes and
  tunnels,
An overhead tangle of wires and airwaves.
But it rests in the lap of the patient earth
Under the gentle gaze of a sky that reaches
  to all eternity.
A city is built in a sacred place.

LIVING AS A COMMUNITY

595 A Safe Place for All

May our town be a safe place:

by day and by night,
for young and for old,
for rich and for poor,
for people of every colour and every faith.

May we be a community.

596 Gathering Together

The seed is Christ's,
The harvest is Christ's;
In the granary of God
May we be gathered.

The sea is Christ's,
The fishes are Christ's;
In the nets of God
May we all meet.

Irish prayer

597 Stopping to Help

Dear God,
When I see someone in trouble,
may I know when to stop and help
and when to hurry to fetch help;
but may I never pass by,
pretending I did not see.

Prayer based on Jesus' parable of the
Good Samaritan, Luke 10:25–37

598 Fellow Human Beings

O God,
We are all strangers in this world
and we are all travelling to your country.

So may we not treat anyone as a foreigner
   or an outsider,
but simply as a fellow human being
made in your image.

599 Respect for Old People

O God,
Help us to respect old people
because it is right to do so.

Help us to show them kindness,
knowing that each and every one of us
is slowly growing old.

600 Graffiti

Not far from where I live
someone has scrawled graffiti on
   a crumbling wall.
"End the injustice NOW!"
But they have vandalized what belongs
   to the community.
If what they have done is unjust,
how can they be working for justice?

So I will not be spraying graffiti.
I will say invisible prayers to God in heaven,
and in so doing be strengthened to work
   for justice
in ways that are kind and humble and
   unseen.

601 Owning Up

O God,
The police are looking for the people
    who did the crime.
They're saying it was probably kids.
They're probably right.
It was probably the ones I was with
    that day.
I think I might have been there.
I think I might have been part of it.

O God,
It's hard to go up to anyone and say,
"Oh, you know that crime everyone's
    talking about. Well, I was part of it."
You see, it wasn't meant to be a crime.
It was meant to be just a bit of messing
    about.
It wasn't meant to go wrong.

O God,
How am I even going to begin to put
    things right?
What if it's only me who gets into
    trouble?
I'm not the only one to blame!
What if I get everyone into trouble?
I can't just tell on them.

But now I've made up my mind:
I'm going to have to do the hard thing.
I'm going to have to go and find someone
   and say,
"Oh, you know that crime everyone's talking
   about. Well, I was part of it."

O God,
Help me with what happens after that.

602 Homeless

The man on the pavement was shivering, Lord,
the man, he was shivering with cold;
the frost in the air made his hair look grey,
his eyes were sunken and old.

I didn't know what I should do, dear Lord,
and still don't know what I can give
to help that man get up and walk away
to where he can laugh and live.

603 For Those Who Have No Home

Dear God,
I pray for those who have no home,
who walk the streets,
who trudge the roads.
I pray for those who want to help them
with the door of welcome
and the meal of companionship
and the bed of rest.
May they bring blessings to each other.

604 Helping in Little Ways

We see people in need
and do not know how to help.
The problem seems too big.

Show us how to begin to help
in little ways.

605 Surviving in the City

God of the city,
God of the street,
help us survive
all the dangers we meet.

God of the city
in heaven above,
may we bring this place
your justice and love.

606 For Victims of Crime

Dear God,
Be very close to people who have been hurt
by crime.
Help them in their shock and helplessness
and shower them with kindness and love.

607 Let Us Not Pass By

When Jesus came to Golgotha they hanged
   him on a tree,
They drove great nails through hand and
   foot, and made a Calvary;
They crowned him with a crown of thorns,
   red were his wounds and deep,
For those were crude and cruel days, and
   human flesh was cheap.

When Jesus came to Birmingham they
   simply passed him by,
They never hurt a hair of him, they only
   let him die;
For men had grown more tender, and they
   would not give him pain;
They only just passed down the street,
   and left him in the rain.

Still Jesus cried, "Forgive them for they
   know not what they do,"
And still it rained – a wintry rain that
   drenched him through and through.
The crowds went home and left the streets
   without a soul to see,
And Jesus crouched against a wall and
   cried for Calvary.

G.A. Studdert Kennedy (1883–1929)

608 A City Pilgrim

I am a city pilgrim:
with God I walk the street,
looking for the face of Christ
in everyone I meet.

609 Newcomers

O God,
Help us to make room in our community
for newcomers.

Help us to make room in our school
for newcomers.

Help us to make room in our hearts
for newcomers.

610 A Home for Everyone

O God,
May our town be a home and garden
   for everyone.

Under our feet, let there be both smooth
   paths and green lawns.
All around, let there be both clean buildings
   and pleasant spaces.
Above us, let there be roofs to shelter us
   and a view to your blue heaven.

611 Working for a Safe Community

We pray for the people who work to keep
us safe in our community:

the police officers who deal with troublemakers;
the ambulance drivers who rush to help
   the sick and injured;
the firefighters who come to help and
   to rescue.

We give thanks for their dedication and their
bravery.

Help us to play our part in making our
community a safe place to be.

612 Doing Our Part

O Lord, let us not live to be useless,
for Christ's sake.

John Wesley (1703–88)

613 Crossing the Road

Thank you, dear God,
for the people who help us cross the
    road to school:
when the sun is bright,
when the clouds are low,
when the wind blows fiercely,
when the rain pelts down.

May we remember to thank them,
our all-weather friends.

614 People Who Help Us

Thank you, dear God, for the many people
who help us when we are out and about:

those who are extra helpful in making sure
we don't get lost;

those who are extra watchful to make sure
we stay out of danger;

those who are extra kind in making sure
we get home safely.

Thank you, dear God, for the many
strangers who are not a danger, but a
blessing.

615 Working in Hospital

Kind Jesus,
Give strength to those who work
   in hospitals:
helping the lame to walk
and the blind to see
and restoring the sick to health.
Bless their work of healing.

616 For the Government

Dear God,
Guide those who govern this country.
May they make wise choices.
May they bear in mind the needs of
young and old, rich and poor, men and
women, people born in this country
and those from overseas.
May their decisions help everyone to live
their lives usefully, happily, and at peace
with one another.

617 For Minorities

Dear God,
We pray for minorities: for the little
groups of people whose needs are
overlooked; the people whose voices are
not heard; the people who do not have
much power.

Help us to find ways to help them in
our community. Help us to find ways
to make the government notice them.
Help us to work for justice in our own
country.

618 For the Blessing of the Old and New

Thank you, dear God,
for the blessing of things that stay the same:
for people we have known for ever
and the familiar paths where we walk.

Thank you, dear God,
for the blessing of things that change:
for newcomers with their new customs,
new ways of doing things, new paths
  to discover.

Thank you, dear God,
for the blessing of the old and the blessing
  of the new.

15 A World in Need

619 Sharing

We share the earth
we share the sky
we share the shining sea
with those we trust
with those we fear:
we are God's family.

620 Heal the World

Heal the world's sorrows
Dry the world's tears
Calm the world's worries
End the world's fears.

FREEDOM

621 Respecting Others

May all the peoples of the world be free to
believe what they believe and to live as they
want to live, while respecting what others
believe and how others want to live.

622 Better Ways

All over the world governments are doing
things that would not be allowed in our
school: stealing what belongs to others…
sending gangs to beat up the people they
don't like… refusing to own up to what
they have done.

O God, send someone to stop them,
someone to help them learn better ways.

623 Broken Bits

Father, take all the broken bits of our lives:
Our broken promises;
Our broken friendships;
Our differences of opinion;
Our different backgrounds, and shapes
    and sizes;
And arrange them together,
Fitting them into each other to make
    something beautiful
Like an artist makes a stained glass window.
Make a design
Your design
Even when all we can see are the broken
    bits.

Anonymous

624 Different Points of View

May we learn to appreciate different
points of view:

to know that the view from the hill is
   different from the view in the valley;
the view to the east is different from the
   view to the west;
the view in the morning is different from
   the view in the evening;
the view of a parent is different from the
   view of a child;
the view of a friend is different from the
   view of a stranger;
the view of humankind is different from
   the view of God.

May we all learn to see what is good, what
is true, what is worthwhile.

625 Tolerance

O God, help us not to despise or oppose
what we do not understand.

William Penn (1644–1718)

JUSTICE

626 Taking Care of Me

All around the world there are people
taking care of me.

They grow my food, they stitch my
clothes, they make everything I use
at school from colouring crayons to
computers.

I don't know their names. I don't know
anything about what they eat or what
they wear or what kind of things they
have in their schools.

In fact, I only know the names of their
countries from the labels, and I know
that in some of those countries, many
people are quite poor.

It's nice that they take care of me, but
I wonder: am I taking care of them in
the price I pay for all they do?

Because people should be fair to one
another; and I want to be fair to them.

627 I Think of the Prisoner

I think of the prisoner, sighing in their cell.

Once, they were a child like me:
running for the joy of running,
singing for the joy of singing,
laughing for the joy of laughing.

O God, unlock the door that holds them
in misery.

628 Good Things and Bad Things

O God,
I do not understand
why bad things happen to good people;
but I want to learn to do good things,
even to bad people.

629 Prayer for Justice

O God,
How long must I call for help
before you listen?
How can you let this wrongdoing go on…
all the fighting and the quarrelling?
Wicked people are getting the better of
good people; it is not right, it is not fair! …

I will wait quietly for God to bring justice.
Even in the middle of disaster I will be
joyful, because God is my saviour.

Based on the book of Habakkuk

630 Turning Away

May I turn away from greed.
May we all turn away from greed.
May God help us all to live in peace.

May I turn away from prejudice.
May we all turn away from prejudice.
May God help us all to live in peace.

May I turn away from violence.
May we all turn away from violence.
May God help us all to live in peace.

631 Gather Us Together

O God,
Gather together as one
those who believe in peace.
Gather together as one
those who believe in justice.
Gather together as one
those who believe in love.

632 Those Whose Life is Hard

I climb into my soft bed
and remember those whose life is hard;
I snuggle under my warm quilt
and remember those whose life is cold;
I lay my head down upon my pillow
and pray that you will give us all rest.

633 In the Face of Evil

In the face of evil and wrongdoing
I will surely not be happy,
Nor will I let myself grow too sad.
Instead, I will choose to stand up for
   what is right
And I will face the future
With calm and courage and cheerfulness.

634 There Will Be Justice One Day

There will be justice one day,
I know it.

There will be some great judgment day,
when everyone will assemble before God,
and God will look at each person in turn,
into their eyes, into their heart, into their
    soul,
and God will know even better than they do
what there is within them that is good
and what there is within them that is
    wicked.
And God will cleanse them with a pure,
    fierce justice
and forgive with a kind and gentle love.

There will be justice one day,
I know it.

635 Goodness and Happiness

Dear God, I believe in goodness:
I believe it is stronger than badness.

Dear God, I believe in happiness:
I believe it is stronger than sadness.

636 Prayer for Change

May the world turn round about,
may all things turn to right;
may the sunset thank the dawn,
the noontime bless the night;

May the rivers thank the rain,
the stormclouds bless the sea;
may the good soil thank the leaves,
the sunshine bless the tree;

May the rich thank those in need,
the children bless the old;
may the strong thank those who fail,
the timid bless the bold;

May the angels sing on earth,
may heaven hear our prayer;
may forgiveness, joy and peace
and love fill everywhere.

637 For Those Known by Their Number

I say a prayer
for those who are known by their number:

prisoners in their cells;
refugees in the campgrounds;
victims of war and of famine.

Dear God,
Speak to each of them
and call them by their name.

638 For Those Condemned as Wicked

We pray for the people who are condemned
  as wicked:
those who are responsible for wars and
massacres and terrorism.

We pray that people of good faith will find
a way to stop them.

We also pray that you and we will treat them
with justice and mercy.

PEACE

639 Peace in My World

Peace in my heart.
Peace in my home.
Peace in my street.
Peace in my world.

640 Prayer for the World

World without love,
World without peace:

Be filled with God's love,
Be filled with God's peace.

641 Ours to Share

The sand on the shore is ours to share
until the tide sweeps in;
the land of the earth is ours to share
until time rolls away.
We share the sand,
we share the land,
O God, bring us your peace.

642 Children of War

We pray for the children
Who were born to know war
Who were born to know grief
Who were born to know violence.

May they learn gentleness
May they learn joy
May they learn peace.

643 Peace Where There is War

Where the bombs are falling
let there be only rain.

Where the bullets are whistling
let there be only wind.

Where the wars have left the land bleak
  and bare
let there be a springtime of peace.

644 Prayer for World Peace

God our Father, Creator of the world,
please help us to love one another.
Make nations friendly with other nations;
make all of us love one another like brothers
    and sisters.
Help us to do our part to bring peace in
    the world
and happiness to all people.

Prayer from Japan

645 Settle the Quarrels

O God,
Settle the quarrels among the nations.

May they hammer their swords into ploughs
and their spears into pruning knives...

Where the tanks now roll, let there be tractors;
where the landmines explode, let the fields
    grow crops.

Let there be a harvest of fruit and grain
and peace that all the world can share.

Based on Micah 4:3–5

646 Prayer for Courage

Dear God,
Give us the courage to overcome anger
with love.

647 Children at War

Dear God,
We think of the children who have to go
to war today, when they would rather be
at school.

Lead them to a safe place where they can
lay down their weapons and learn to be
children again.

648 Heirs of Peace

O God, make us children of quietness
and heirs of peace.

St Clement (1st century)

649 Trust and Friendship

May the things I say
help to build trust and friendship.

May the things I do
help to build trust and friendship.

May I set my heart
to build trust and friendship.

650 Prayer for the Casualties of War

Dear God,
We pray for the casualties of war:

for the young and the old,
for the parents and the children;

for the birds and the animals,
for the fields and the flowers;

for the earth and the water,
for the sea and the sky.

We pray for their healing.

651 **Strengthen Us**

Strengthen us, O God, to relieve the
oppressed, to hear the groans of poor
prisoners, to reform the abuses of all
professions; that many be made not poor
to make a few rich; for Jesus Christ's sake.

From a letter of Oliver Cromwell (1599–1658)

652 **Prayer for Calm**

Shield us from violence,
Shield us from harm,
Find for us a shelter
Of quiet and of calm.

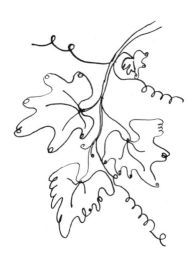

653 Bringing Down the Wall

Why is there a wall between us –
Wall of concrete, wall of wire,
Wall of deeply rooted hatred,
Wall of angry bullet fire?

On the wall I write a poem:
Words of hope and words of peace;
On your side, you paint a picture
Of the time when war will cease.

On that day, we'll bring you flowers;
You'll bring fruit grown in your land.
We will celebrate together –
Sisters, brothers, hand in hand.

654 Wish

Peace in the day:

Peace in my school
Peace in my home
Peace in the world.

Peace in the night:

Peace in the world
Peace in my home
Peace in my heart.

655 The Olive Tree

The olive tree I thought was dead
has opened new green leaves instead
and where the landmines tore the earth
now poppies dance with joy and mirth.

The doves build nests, they coo and sigh
beside the fields where corn grows high
and grapes hang heavy on the vine,
and those who fought share bread and wine.

656 Prayer for Healing

Dear God,
Mend the lives of those damaged by war:
heal their wounds
and heal their hearts.

657 Prayer for Living Together in Peace

May all the peoples of the world have a
place where they can make their home.
May they live without quarrel.
May they live without enmity.
May they live in freedom and prosper.

From the story of Isaac, Genesis 26

658 The Seeds of Peace

In the fields of war
let us sow the seeds of peace.

REFUGEES

659 The World's Family

O God,
We remember those who have no house
   to call their home.
Give them shelter.

We remember those who have no country
   to call their home.
Give them refuge.

May we remember that we belong to the
   world's great family
and find a way to help them, our brothers
   and sisters.

660 Prayer for Refugees

Lord, watch over refugees,
their tired feet aching.
Help them bear their heavy loads,
their backs breaking.
May they find a place of rest,
no fears awake them.
May you always be their guide,
never forsake them.

FAMINE AND DISASTER

661 Trouble in the Fields

There's trouble in the fields, Lord,
The crops are parched and dry.
We water them with tears, Lord,
So help us, hear our cry.

There's trouble in our hearts, Lord,
The world is full of pain.
Set us to work for healing,
Send blessings down like rain.

662 Prayer for Harvest Crops

Lord, help those who plant and sow,
weed and water, rake and hoe,
toiling in the summer heat
for the food they need to eat.

Bless the work of their tired hands:
turn their dry and dusty lands
to a garden, green and gold,
as their harvest crops unfold.

663 Send Healing Rain

Dear God,
Send healing rain
to the dusty lands,
to the dry lands,
to the hungry lands.

664 Prayer for Those Afflicted by Drought

Drought and disaster
had stripped the land bare,
now God's harvest blessings
grow new everywhere:
the wheat fields are gold,
there are grapes on the vine;
let's meet at the table
to share bread and wine.

Based on Amos 9

665 Give Strength to Brave Helpers

Give strength, dear God, to the brave people
who go to help places that are torn apart by
    disasters.
Keep them safe.
Help them to know what is the right thing
    to do.
Turn their efforts into miracles.

666 God's Love and Goodness

Dear God,
When everything is going wrong I sometimes
wonder why you let bad things happen.

But then you open my eyes to the majesty
of your world, and I know once more that
you are far greater than I can imagine, and
I believe once more that your love and
goodness will not be overcome.

Based on the book of Job

16 God Our Creator

667 The God of All

Our God is the God of all,
The God of heaven and earth,
Of the sea and the rivers;
The God of the sun and of the moon and
    of all the stars;
The God of the lofty mountains and of the
    lowly valleys,
He has His dwelling around heaven and
    earth, and sea, and all that in them is.

St Patrick (389–461)

668 Glory to God

Glory to God for everything!

St John Chrysostom (347–407)

Belief

669 I Believe

Dear God,
I believe in you.

Some people laugh
but I will not be ashamed.

Some people tease
but I will not grow afraid.

Some people praise
but I will not grow proud.

Dear God,
I believe in you
and I just want to grow wise.

670 Angels and Miracles

Even if I do not see an angel,
may I hear what God has to say to me;
even if I do not see a miracle,
may I understand what God is doing for me.

671 Let Us Know God

O gracious and holy Father,
give us wisdom to perceive thee,
intelligence to understand thee,
diligence to seek thee,
patience to wait for thee,
eyes to behold thee,
a heart to meditate upon thee,
and a life to proclaim thee;
through the power of the Spirit of Jesus
Christ our Lord.

Attributed to St Benedict (480–543)

672 The Beauty of the World

Because of the beauty of the world
I believe in the Maker God.

673 The Greatness of God

Do not think that the sun is brighter than
God is, or equal to him: for the one who
created the sun must be immeasurably
greater and brighter.

*Based on words by St Cyril of
Jerusalem (c. 315–387)*

674 Imagine the Maker God

Think of the tiniest of tiny, tiny things.
Think of the hugest of huge, enormous things.

Imagine the God who made the tiny things.
Imagine the God who made the huge things.

Just imagine: the Maker God.

675 Understanding

I am too little to understand even the
everyday things that grown-ups understand;
so I am not surprised that I do not
understand how or why the world exists
and what everything is all about.

But I do understand that where there is love
there is happiness and everything seems as it
should be.

676 Let My Faith Grow

Dear God,
My faith is no bigger than a seed.
Let it grow into a tree.

677 Faith, Hope and Love

I believe that faith can revive the world.
I believe that hope can renew the world.
I believe that love can redeem the world.

O God, give us faith and hope and love.

678 Hope

All my hope on God is founded;
he doth still my trust renew.
Me through change and chance he guideth,
only good and only true.
God unknown,
he alone
calls my heart to be his own.

*Joachim Neander (1650–80), freely adapted
by Robert Bridges (1844–1930)*

679 My Candle Burns

My candle burns; its tiny light
shines to make this dark place bright.

My candle burns, a flame of love,
shining up to heaven above.

680 River of Love

Move our hearts with the calm, smooth flow
of your grace. Let the river of your love run
through our souls. May my soul be carried
by the current of your love, towards the wide,
infinite ocean of heaven.

Gilbert of Hoyland (12th century)

681 The Wide Everywhere

I don't feel afraid
to look up to the sky
and its miles and miles of blue;
for in the clear air
and the wide everywhere
is the love that surrounds me and you.

682 Trust in God

O Lord, Whose way is perfect,
help us, we pray Thee, always to trust in
 Thy goodness:
that walking with Thee and following Thee
 in all simplicity
we may possess quiet and contented minds
and trust ourselves to the love of our
 heavenly Father
now and evermore.

Christina Rossetti (1830–94)

683 God is the Best Parent

O God,
as truly as you are our father,
so just as truly you are our mother.
We thank you, God our father,
for your strength and goodness.
We thank you, God our mother,
for the closeness of your caring.
O God, we thank you for the great love
you have for each one of us.

Julian of Norwich

684 The Lord Sees Everyone

The Lord has his throne in heaven.
He watches people everywhere
and knows what they are doing.

He sees the wicked, and his heart is
against them.

He sees the righteous and loves their
good deeds.

From Psalm 11

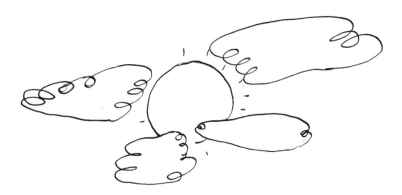

685 Things of God

Three things are of the evil one:
  An evil eye;
  An evil tongue;
  An evil mind.

Three things are of God, and these three
are what Mary told to her Son, for she heard
them in heaven:
  The merciful word,
  The singing word,
  And the good word.

May the power of these three holy things be
on all men and women of Erin for evermore.

Traditional Irish prayer

686 Trust

Teach us, O gracious Lord, to begin our
works with fear, to go on with obedience,
and to finish them in love; and then to
wait patiently in hope, and with cheerful
confidence to look up to thee, whose
promises are faithful and rewards infinite;
through Jesus Christ.

George Hickes (1642–1715)

687 God is Near Me

I know God is always near me
and nothing can shake me.

From Psalm 16

688 God Makes Me Strong

God makes me strong
and keeps my pathway safe;
he makes me sure-footed as a deer
on the perilous mountainside.

From Psalm 18

689 Knowing God's Goodness

I have faith in God
and I believe that I will not have to wait
for heaven to know God's goodness.

From Psalm 27

690 God's Love Lasts For Ever

All things that are on earth shall wholly
    pass away,
Except the love of God, which shall live
    and last for aye.

William C. Bryant (1794–1878)

691 Love as High as the Heavens

Love as high as the heavens,
Justice as deep as the sea,
Righteousness like the mountains:
God is faithful to me.

From Psalm 36

692 May I See Jesus

May I see Jesus:
lying in the manger.

May I see Jesus:
preaching on the hillside.

May I see Jesus:
dying on the cross.

May I see Jesus:
risen from the dead.

May I see Jesus:
ascending into heaven.

May I see Jesus:
returning in glory.

693 Show Thyself to Me

O great God, who art thou? Where art thou?
Show thyself to me.

*Venkayya, first outcaste convert in the Church of South
India; prayer offered every day for three years*

694 I Believe in God

I believe in the sun even when it is not
  shining
I believe in love where feeling is not
I believe in God even if he is silent.

Inscription on the walls of a cellar in Cologne,
Germany, where Jews hid from the Nazis

695 I Am a Child

Dear God,
I am a child.
Welcome me into your kingdom.

Based on Matthew 18:1–5

696 My Offering

I offer thee
Every flower that ever grew,
Every bird that ever flew,
Every wind that ever blew,
  Good God.

I offer thee
Ever wave that ever moved,
Every heart that ever loved,
Thee, my Father's well-beloved,
  Dear Lord.

I offer thee
Every flake of virgin snow,
Every spring of earth below,
Every human joy and woe,
  My Love!

Irish prayer

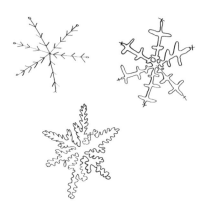

697 Room in My Heart

Thou didst leave thy throne and thy kingly
  crown
When thou camest to earth for me;
But in Bethlehem's home was there found
  no room
For thy holy Nativity.
  O, come to my heart, Lord Jesus;
  There is room in my heart for thee.

Emily E.S. Elliott (1836–97)

698 Christ is Coming Again

The wind from the south means sunshine,
The cloud in the west means rain,
A world in need of salvation
means Christ is coming again.

Based on Luke 12:54–56

699 Open My Mind

Open my mind, O Lord,
to see your light.

Open my mind, O Lord,
to know the hope to which you have
  called me.

Open my mind, O Lord,
to see the wonderful blessings you have
  promised.

Open my mind, O Lord,
to see your power at work in me.

Based on Ephesians 1:18

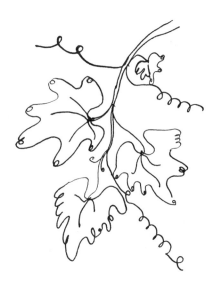

700 God's Love

Since he is wise he loves you with wisdom.
Since he is good he loves you with goodness.
Since he is holy he loves you with holiness.
Since he is just he loves you with justice.
Since he is merciful he loves you with mercy.
Since he is compassionate he loves you with
    compassion.
Since he is gentle he loves you with gentleness.

St John of the Cross (1542–91)

701 Book of Life

O God, write my name in the book of life.

702 Love Me Evermore

O God, I hear you calling me
like someone at my door;
O God, come in and stay with me
and love me evermore.

703 Come!

Come, Lord Jesus!

Revelation 22:20

704 A True Child of God

I am a child,
and I think like a child
and act like a child.

When I am grown-up,
I shall think like a grown-up
and act like a grown-up.

But when at last I see God face to face,
I shall think and act like a true child
of God.

Based on 1 Corinthians 13:11–12

705 You Are My God

You are holy, Lord, the only God,
and your deeds are wonderful.
You are strong.
You are great.
You are the Most High,
You are almighty.
You, holy Father, are
King of heaven and earth.
You are Three and One,
Lord God, all good.
You are Good, all Good, supreme Good,
Lord God, living and true.
You are love,
You are wisdom.
You are humility,
You are endurance.
You are rest,
You are peace.
You are joy and gladness.
You are justice and moderation.
You are all our riches,
And you suffice for us.
You are beauty.
You are gentleness.
You are our protector,
You are our guardian and defender.
You are courage.
You are our haven and our hope.
You are our faith,

Our great consolation.
You are our eternal life,
Great and wonderful Lord,
God almighty,
Merciful Saviour.

St Francis of Assisi (1181–1226)

PRAISE

706 Your Greatness is Seen in All the World

O God, your greatness is seen in all the world!

I look at the sky, which you have made;
at the moon and the stars, which you set
in their places, and I wonder:

Who am I, that you think of me?

What is humankind, that you care for us?

O God, your greatness is seen in all the world!

From Psalm 8:1, 3–4

707 All Things Praise Thee

All things praise thee Lord most high!
Heaven and earth and sea and sky!

Time and space are praising thee!
All things praise thee; Lord, may we!

George William Conder (1821–74)

708 Shout and Sing

Let the whole world shout and sing,
Let your praises joyful ring!
God has come as this world's king:
Peace and justice he will bring.

From Psalm 98

709 Thanking God

Now thank we all our God
With hearts and hands and voices
Who wondrous things hath done,
In whom his world rejoices;
Who from our mother's arms
Hath blessed us on our way
With countless gifts of love,
And still is ours today.

*Martin Rinkart (1586–1649), translated
by Catherine Winkworth (1827–78)*

710 God's Love is Everlasting

Give thanks to the Lord, because he is good;
his love is everlasting.
He alone performs great miracles;
his love is everlasting.
By his wisdom he made the heavens;
his love is everlasting;
he built the earth on the deep waters;
his love is everlasting.
He did not forget us when we were defeated;
his love is everlasting;
he freed us from our enemies;
his love is everlasting.
Give thanks to the God of heaven;
his love is everlasting.

From Psalm 136:1, 4–6, 23–26

711 Ever Faithful, Ever Sure

Let us with a gladsome mind
Praise the Lord for he is kind;
For his mercies ay endure,
Ever faithful, ever sure.

John Milton (1608–74)

712 Praise for God Alone

You alone, O God, deserve praise and glory, because of your constant love and faithfulness.

Psalm 115:1

713 God's Wonderful Works

May none of God's wonderful works keep silence, night or morning. Bright stars, high mountains, the depths of the seas, sources of rushing rivers: may all these break into song as we sing to Father, Son and Holy Spirit. May all the angels in the heavens reply: Amen, Amen, Amen. Power, praise, honour, eternal glory to God, the only Giver of grace, Amen, Amen, Amen.

Anonymous (3rd–6th centuries)

714 Praise from All the World

Praise the Lord!

Praise the Lord from heaven,
    you that live in the heights above.
Praise him, all his angels,
    all his heavenly armies.

Praise him, sun and moon;
    praise him, shining stars.
Praise him, highest heavens,
    and the waters above the sky.

Let them all praise the name of the Lord!
    He commanded, and they were created;
by his command they were fixed in their
    places for ever,
    and they cannot disobey.

Praise the Lord from the earth,
    seamonsters and all ocean depths;
lightning and hail, snow and clouds,
    strong winds that obey his command.

Praise him, hills and mountains,
    fruit trees and forests;
all animals, tame and wild,
    reptiles and birds.

Praise him, kings and all peoples,
  princes and all other rulers;
young women and young men,
  old people and children too.

Let them all praise the name of the Lord!
His name is greater than all others;
  his glory is above earth and heaven.
He made his nation strong,
  so that all his people praise him –
  the people of Israel, so dear to him.

Praise the Lord!

Psalm 148

715 Praising God

I praise the Lord with all my soul,
my strength, my heart, my mind:
he blesses me with love and grace
and is for ever kind.

Based on Psalm 103:1–4

716 **Praise God with Music**

Praise the Lord!

Praise God in his Temple!
  Praise his strength in heaven!
Praise him for the mighty things he has done.
  Praise his supreme greatness.

Praise him with trumpets.
  Praise him with harps and lyres.
Praise him with drums and dancing.
  Praise him with harps and flutes.
Praise him with cymbals.
  Praise him with loud cymbals.
Praise the Lord, all living creatures!

Praise the Lord!

Psalm 150

717 Mary's Song of Praise

My heart praises the Lord;
my soul is glad because of God my Saviour,
for he has remembered me, his lowly
   servant!
From now on all people will call me happy,
because of the great things the Mighty God
   has done for me.
His name is holy.

Part of Mary's song of praise, Luke 1:46–49

718 God Will Redeem Us

Let us praise the Lord!

He will cause the bright dawn of salvation
   to rise on us
and to shine from heaven on all those who
   live in the dark shadow of death,
to guide our steps into the path of peace.

From the prayer of Zechariah,
the father of John the Baptist.
Luke 1:68, 78–79

719 Glory to God

Our Lord and God! You are worthy to
  receive glory, honour and power.
For you created all things,
and by your will they were given existence
  and life.

Revelation 4:11

720 Praise God's Greatness

Honour God, and praise his greatness!

Worship him who made heaven, earth, sea,
and the springs of water!

Words of the Angel of Good News, Revelation 14:7

17 Following God

721 How I Live

Let me live cheerfully
Let me live carefully
Let me live thoughtfully
Let me live prayerfully.

722 Joy

May I have joy in my heart.
May I have joy in my life.
May I bring joy to others.
May I spread joy throughout the world.

GOD IN MY LIFE

723 Walking into the Light

I will turn away from wrong,
I will turn to do what's right;
I will walk out of the dark,
I will walk into the light.

724 More Like Jesus

I'm learning to be more like Jesus,
I'm learning the right way to live.
I'm learning to show loving kindness,
I'm learning to truly forgive.

725 Jesus, Be with Us

Jesus, who walked to the cross,
be with us when we feel abandoned.

Jesus, who walked to the cross,
be with us when we face danger.

Jesus, who walked to the cross,
be with us when we are suffering.

When wickedness threatens to defeat us,
Jesus, who rose from the dead, be with us.

726 Rich, Powerful, Famous

O God,
I want to be rich:
rich like the golden sun,
rich without selfishness.

I want to be powerful:
powerful like the shifting ocean,
powerful without malice.

I want to be famous:
famous like the tallest mountain,
famous for reflecting your glory.

727 A Willing Heart

O Lord our God, give us by thy Holy Spirit
a willing heart and a ready hand
to use all thy gifts to thy praise and glory;
through Jesus Christ our Lord.

Archbishop Cranmer (1489–1556)

728 When to Speak

Dear God,
Help me know when to speak up to tell
the truth,
and when to keep silent so as not to stir
up trouble.

729 A Kind Deed

I did a kind deed for someone else,
I did a kind deed for free;
but I am hoping that when I'm in need
some kindness will come back to me.

730 Shaping My World

Help me shape my dreams:
bless my planning
and my preparing.

Help me shape my here and now:
bless my thinking
and my doing.

Help me shape my memories:
bless my remembering
and my forgetting.

731 Nobody, Somebody

Dear God,
When I feel like a nobody
going nowhere,
make me into a somebody
doing something for you.

732 Seeing God in Others

Teach me, my God and king,
In all things thee to see,
That what I do in anything
To do it as for thee.

George Herbert (1593–1632)

733 Secrets

Dear God,
may I keep secret those things that can
   be kept secret;
may I tell the secrets that should be told.

734 A Worthwhile Life

Dear God,
I sometimes wonder how long I will live.
Will it be many years?
Will it be few?
However many years you give me, dear God,
enable me to fit into them
a whole and worthwhile life.

735 Open My Eyes

Open my eyes
so I can see
the ways I could
more useful be.

Give me the strength
and heart and mind
to do the things
that are good and kind.

736 The Ways of Heaven

Dear God,
I am newly arrived on earth.
Help me learn the ways of the world.
But I will stay here only one lifetime.
Let me begin now to learn the ways
of heaven.

737 Here and Now

I could perhaps plant a garden of trees
but it would not be paradise.

I could perhaps build a city of gold
but it would not be the holy city.

But here and now I can follow Jesus
and in this way God's kingdom will grow.

738 Good Deeds

May all my deeds
be wheat
not weeds.

739 Right and True

May I learn to say what is right and true
without anger and without spitefulness.

740 Patience

Dear God,
I need to become more patient. Please help
me to change my ways as soon as possible.

741 Make Us to Walk in Your Way

Lord, make us to walk in your way:
"Where there is love and wisdom,
there is neither fear nor ignorance;
where there is patience and humility,
there is neither anger nor annoyance;
where there is poverty and joy, there is
neither greed nor avarice; where there
is peace and contemplation, there is
neither care nor restlessness; where
there is the fear of God to guard the
dwelling, there no enemy can enter;
where there is mercy and prudence,
there is neither excess nor harshness";
this we know through your Son,
Jesus Christ our Lord.

St Francis of Assisi (1181–1226)

742 Doing What is Right

Dear God,
I resolve this day to do what is right,
even if no one else will join me.

743 God, Protect Me

Drive from me every temptation and danger,
Surround me on the sea of unrighteousness,
And in the narrows, crooks, and straits,
Keep thou my coracle, keep it always.

From Carmina Gadelica

744 Boasting About Goodness

Dear God,
May I never boast of doing good.

Some people boast about the good things
they have done, and others gather round
to cheer and make them feel important.

Help me to do good for the sake of goodness
itself.

745 Doing God's Will

Teach us, Lord,
to serve you as you deserve,
to give and not to count the cost,
to fight and not to heed the wounds,
to toil and not to seek for rest,
to labour and not to ask for any reward
save that of knowing that we do your will.

St Ignatius Loyola (1491–1556)

746 The Struggle to Do Good

Doing good sometimes feels like struggling
uphill, with an avalanche of mischief
crashing all around; but other times it
feels like paddling down the river of
righteousness, towards the great sea
of everlasting kindness.

747 If You Love, You Will Be Loved

If you love, you will be loved.
If you serve, you will be served.
If you fear, you will be feared.
If you do good to others, it is right
that others should do good to you.
Blessed is the one who truly loves
and does not ask to be loved in return.
Blessed is the one who serves and
does not ask to be served.
Blessed is the one who fears and
does not ask to be feared.
Blessed is the one who does good to
others and does not ask that others
do good in return.

Based on words by Brother Giles (died 1251)

748 Everything I Do

May everything I do be a sacrament to
    gentleness
A step to the horizon land of white and gold
A seed that I sow in the earth of everlastingness
Reaching up to heaven as its leaves unfold.

749 A Safe Place to Go

Dear God,
When people shout in anger
help me to speak calmly.

When people threaten to hit me and hurt me
keep me from striking back.

When people try to lead me into a world of
   wrongdoing
give me the strength to walk away and a safe
   place to go:

a place of refuge,
a place of healing,
a place of forgiveness.

Sophie Piper

750 Ambition

O God
I am ambitious for my life.
I want it to count for something.

So make me ambitious to do good,
to make the world kinder, fairer, lovelier.

751 Small Things with Great Love

We can do no great things,
Only small things with great love.

Mother Teresa of Calcutta (1910–97)

752 Treasures for Heaven

O God,
if I were rich,
very rich,
then I would buy beautiful things,
strong things,
wonderful things –
things to outlast my lifetime,
things that would shine in heaven.
O God,
make me rich enough
to buy treasures for heaven.

753 Just Enough

Dear God,
I have begun to understand why people
long to be rich.

It is because they can buy things so lovely
they can feel they are living in heaven here
in this world.

But I have noticed that even the rich grow
old, and they too must say goodbye to
everything, and there is nothing they can
take with them.

So teach me to be happy with just enough:
enough for myself and enough to share;
enough to help me walk through this
world to your heaven.

754 Living My Life Carefully

Dear God,
Help me to walk carefully
so I do not crush the flowers I see along
  my way.

Help me to talk carefully
so I do not crush the people I meet along
  my way.

Help me to listen carefully
so I do not crush your voice speaking to
  me along my way.

INSPIRATION FROM THE BIBLE

755 Do Not Follow the Wicked

Do not follow the advice of the wicked,
but obey every word of God.

For the wicked are nothing more than
wisps of straw in the autumn gale; but the
righteous are like trees that grow by the
lifegiving river, bearing leaves and fruit in
their season.

From Psalm 1

756 In God's Presence

Who may come into God's presence?

The person who obeys God in everything,
who always speaks the truth,
who keeps every promise,
who cannot be lured into doing wrong.

Such a person will be safe all through life.

From Psalm 15

757 Turn Away from Evil

Come, my young friends, and listen to me,
and I will teach you to honour the Lord.
Would you like to enjoy life?
Do you want long life and happiness?
Then hold back from speaking evil
and from telling lies.
Turn away from evil and do good;
strive for peace with all your heart.

Psalm 34:11–14

758 Trust in the Lord

Trust in the Lord and do good.

Psalm 37:3

759 I Will Obey Your Law

O God,
I will obey your law
for ever and ever.

Psalm 119:44

760 **Your Word is Light**

O God,
Your word is a lamp to guide me
and a light for my path.

Psalm 119:105

761 **Constant Love**

Teach me, O God,
to do what is just,
to show constant love
and to live in fellowship with you.

Based on Micah 6:8

762 **The Right Way to Go**

Dear God,
Help me to find the right way to go,
even though the gate to it be narrow,
and the path difficult to walk.

Based on Matthew 7:13

763 Listening to God

Dear God,
Help me to listen to what you have to say
to me.

May the Evil One not snatch the message
away.

May troubles not cause me to stop
following you.

May worrying about material things not
choke out my longing for holiness.

May I grow and flourish in your kingdom.

Based on the parable of the sower,
Matthew 13:1–24

764 Loving God and Others

Dear God,
Help me to love you with all my heart,
with all my soul and with all my mind.

Help me to love those around me as
much as I love myself.

Based on the words of Jesus
from Matthew 22:34–40

765 Seeing Jesus in Others

Lord Jesus,
Make me as kind to others
as I would want to be to you.

Make me as generous to others
as I would want to be to you.

May I take time to help them
as I would want to take time to help you.

May I take trouble to help them
as I would want to take trouble to help you.

May I look into the faces of those I meet
and see your face.

Based on Matthew 25:37–40

766 Telling Others of Jesus

May the words I speak
tell others of Jesus.

May the things I do
tell others of Jesus.

May my whole life
tell others of Jesus.

Based on James

767 One of God's Friends

Dear God,
Help me to love other people so well that
they recognize me as one of your friends.

Based on John 13:34–35

768 Helping, Encouraging, Forgiving

May we help one another
to follow Jesus;

May we encourage one another
to follow Jesus;

May we forgive one another
as Jesus forgives us.

Based on Romans 12

769 Showing God's Love

Help me, Lord, to show your love.

Help me to be patient and kind, not
jealous or conceited or proud. May I
never be ill-mannered, selfish or irritable;
may I be quick to forgive and forget.

May I not gloat over wrongdoing, but
rather be glad about things that are good
and true.

May I never give up loving: may my faith
and hope and patience never come to an
end.

Based on 1 Corinthians 13:4–7

770 Spirit of God

Spirit of God
put love in my life.

Spirit of God
put joy in my life.

Spirit of God
put peace in my life.

Spirit of God
make me patient.

Spirit of God
make me kind.

Spirit of God
make me good.

Spirit of God
give me faithfulness.

Spirit of God
give me humility.

Spirit of God
give me self-control.

From Galatians 5:22–23

771 May My Life Shine

May my life shine
like a star in the night,
filling my world
with goodness and light.

From Philippians 2:15

772 A New Me

I've taken off the old me
and thrown it all away;
I'm going to be the new me
as from this very day.

Based on Colossians 3:9

773 Choosing Wisely

When I have to choose
between right and wrong
help me make the right choice
and give me peace in my heart.

From Colossians 3:15

774 Doing Good

Dear God,
May I never grow tired of doing good.

From 2 Thessalonians 3:13

775 Belonging to God

The solid foundation that God has laid
cannot be shaken; and on it are written these
words: "The Lord knows those who are his"
and "whoever says that he belongs to the
Lord must turn away from wrongdoing."

From 2 Timothy 2:19

776 Asking God for Goodness

Dear God,
Help me to grow up good.

Help me not to make mistakes just because
I am young.

Help me to be righteous without being smug;
faithful to you without being narrow-minded;
loving without being naïve;
peaceable without being weak.

Help me, dear God, because I ask you.

Based on 2 Timothy 2:22

777 Being Gentle

Dear God,
Help me not to speak evil of anyone, but to
be peaceful and friendly, and always to show
a gentle attitude towards everyone.

From Titus 3:2

778 Hearing God's Word

O God,
May I hear your word.
May I obey your word.

From James 1:22–24

779 Being Holy

God is holy.
God calls us to be holy.

From 1 Peter 1:16

780 Striving to Be Better

To faith, let me add goodness;
to goodness, let me add knowledge;
to knowledge, let me add self-control;
to self-control, let me add endurance;
to endurance, let me add godliness;
to godliness, let me add affection for
    my brothers and sisters;
to affection, let me add love.

From 2 Peter 1:5–7

781 Loving One Another

God is love:
let us learn to love one another.

From 1 John 4:7

782 Obeying God's Laws

O Lord,
I have heard your laws.

May I worship you.

May I worship you alone.

May all I say and do show respect for
your holy name.

May I honour the weekly day of rest.

May I show respect for my parents.

May I reject violence so that I never take
a life.

May I learn to be loyal in friendship and
so learn to be faithful in marriage.

May I not steal what belongs to others.

May I not tell lies to destroy another
person's reputation.

May I not be envious of what others have,
but may I learn to be content with the
good things you give me.

Based on the Ten Commandments, Exodus 20

783 Be with Me

O God,
I will go where you lead me
and I will obey your laws.

Be with me wherever I go
and bring me success in all I do.

Based on Exodus 33

784 Fill My Life with Riches

O God,
Fill my life with true riches:
with wisdom,
with righteousness,
with justice.

Based on Proverbs 8:12

785 Make Me Good

Dear God,
Make me good
so I can be a blessing to others.

Based on Proverbs 10:7

786 Kind Words

Righteous people know the kind thing to say,
but the wicked are always saying things
    that hurt.

O God,
Make me righteous,
make me kind.

First verse: Proverbs 10:32

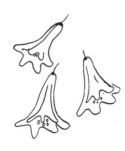

787 Make Me Your Child

O God make me good.
Make me wise.
Make me hardworking.
Make me honest.
Make me tactful.
Make me generous.
Make me truthful.
Make me loyal.
But most of all,
dear God,
make me your child.

Based on Proverbs

788 What I Do

Dear God,
Even though I am only a child
people can tell what I am like
by what I do.

Please make me honest and good.

Based on Proverbs 20:11

789 May God Never Leave Us

May God be with us in this generation,
as he was in past generations.
May he never leave us or abandon us.
May he make us obedient to him,
so that we always live as he wants us to live,
and keep all the laws and commands he
    gave so long ago.

Based on the prayer of King Solomon,
1 Kings 8:57–58

790 Always Ready

Lord Jesus,
may I always be ready to greet you
when it is time to meet you.

Based on Mark 13:37

18 Prayer

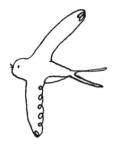

791 Here I Am

Here I am beneath the sky
and all alone in prayer;
but I know God is listening,
for God is everywhere.

792 Angels Singing

Lord, make my heart a place where
angels sing!

John Keble (1792–1866)

HOPING AND PRAYING

793 Can You Hear My Prayer?

O God,
I sometimes wonder
if you are really there.
I wonder, if I wonder,
can you still hear my prayer?

794 Just in Case

I say a prayer without truly believing:
I say a prayer just in case
there is a God who will guard and guide me
and bless me with love and grace.

795 Prayer to the Holy Spirit

Holy Spirit, prompt us
When we kneel to pray;
Nearer come, and teach us
What we ought to say.

Holy Spirit, help us
Daily, by thy might,
What is wrong to conquer,
And to choose the right.

W.H. Parker (1845–1929)

796 I'm Sitting and Thinking

I'm sitting
and thinking
and wondering
and wishing
and dreaming
and hoping
and praying

and hoping
and dreaming
and truly
believing
that God
can hear all
that I'm saying.

797 Like a Kite

There you are, God:
I have written my prayer.
I have arranged the words carefully
and checked the spelling
and written it out neatly.

There it sits on the paper
perfectly crafted
but like a kite on a still day.

Send me faith
like a lively breeze
to take it dancing up to heaven.

798 Help Me Pray!

O God,
It is so hard to keep my mind on my
prayers. My thoughts just run away in
a butterfly meadow of daydreams.
Bring me back to the path that will
lead me into your presence.

799 I Cast My Prayer

I cast my prayer on the river
and let it float to the sea
and over the far horizon
and off to eternity.

800 Prayer for Solitude

Dear God,
Let me find a place where I can be
alone to think.

801 Listening for God

I sit and listen for God.

Sometimes I only hear my own prayers,
echoing back under an empty sky.

Other times I hear a thought from God:
silent, and yet clearer than the sweet,
pure notes of the blackbird.

Sometimes I know I am in the company
of angels, dancing and laughing in a
waterfall of joy.

802 Make My Heart Still

O make my heart so still, so still,
When I am deep in prayer,
That I might hear the white mist-wreaths
Losing themselves in air!

Utsonomya San, Japan

803 Think of the Wind

Think of the wind
howling through the trees.

Think of the wind
singing over the river.

Think of the wind
sighing through the grasses.

Think of the air
standing still and silent,
listening for God.

TRUSTING IN GOD

804 Give Us Grace

Give us grace, Almighty Father, to address thee with all our hearts as well as with our lips.

Thou art everywhere present: from thee no secrets can be hidden.

Teach us to fix our thoughts on thee, reverently and with love, so that our prayers are not in vain, but are acceptable to thee, now and always; through Jesus Christ our Lord.

Jane Austen (1775–1817)

805 Candle Prayer

A tiny light
A tiny prayer
For God's blessing
Everywhere.

806 A Life of Prayer

The prayer of speaking
The prayer of listening

The prayer of kneeling
The prayer of walking

The prayer of working
The prayer of playing

The prayer of giving
The prayer of receiving

The prayer of laughing
The prayer of weeping

The prayer of loving
The prayer of forgiving

The prayer of living
Till life's ending.

807 Prayer to the Trinity

God the Father,
high in heaven,
hear our prayers
and come close to us.

God the Son,
high in heaven,
hear our prayers
and come close to us.

God the Holy Spirit,
high in heaven,
hear our prayers
and come close to us.

808 A Child's Prayer

Lord, teach a little child to pray,
    And then accept my prayer,
Thou hearest all the words I say
    For thou art everywhere.

A little sparrow cannot fall
    Unnoticed, Lord, by thee,
And though I am so young and small
    Thou dost take care of me.

Teach me to do the thing that's right,
   And when I sin, forgive,
And make it still my chief delight
   To serve thee while I live.

Jane Taylor (1783–1824)

809 **Prayer Without Words**

Dear God,
You know what I want to pray
so I shan't bother you with the words.

810 **Time to Pray**

Dear God,
I have come to this quiet room.
I have closed the door.
I have come to pray.

Based on Matthew 6:5

811 The Prayer Jesus Taught

Our Father in heaven:
May your holy name be honoured;
may your Kingdom come;
may your will be done on earth as
   it is in heaven.
Give us today the food we need.
Forgive us the wrongs we have done,
as we forgive the wrongs that others
   have done to us.
Do not bring us to hard testing,
but keep us safe from the Evil One.

Matthew 6:9–13

Father:
May your holy name be honoured;
may your kingdom come.
Give us day by day the food we need.
Forgive us our sins,
for we forgive everyone who does us wrong.
And do not bring us to hard testing.

Luke 11:2–4

Our Father in heaven,
hallowed be your name,
your kingdom come,
your will be done,
on earth as in heaven.
Give us today our daily bread.
Forgive us our sins
as we forgive those who sin against us.
Lead us not into temptation
but deliver us from evil.
For the kingdom, the power,
and the glory are yours
now and for ever.
Amen

The Lord's Prayer

812 Different Kinds of Prayer

Some prayers are like a still green pool:
sitting quietly.

Some prayers are like a slow river:
talking solemnly.

Some prayers are like a mountain stream:
laughing joyfully.

813 Prayers of the Seasons

Some prayers seem to belong
  in spring meadows:
full of hope.

Some prayers seem to belong
  by the summer ocean:
full of joy.

Some prayers seem to belong
  to the autumn forest:
full of wisdom.

Some prayers seem to belong
  to the winter wasteland:
full of pain.

All these prayers belong to God:
God of the changing years.

19 Forgiveness

814 Love Heals

O God,
The wrong I have done
now makes me sad;

The love that you give
will make me glad.

SORRY AND CONFUSED

815 Mischief

Dear God,
I haven't been wicked.
I'm not evil inside.
I'm just a bit mischievous.
I am sorry for upsetting people
but I am also feeling sorry for myself.
Please help.

816 Clumsiness

Dear God,
Please help grown-ups to understand the
difference between being clumsy and being
naughty. I am sad about being clumsy but
I am not sorry about being naughty,
because I wasn't.

817 Not Sorry

Dear God,
Please forgive me for saying sorry when
I wasn't. Please forgive me for not feeling
sorry even now. Please help me untangle
my muddled feelings.

818 Pretending

Dear God,
I am not yet ready to say sorry for what
I did because I am still trying to pretend
that I did not do it.

819 Misunderstood

Dear God,
In my heart I believe I have done no wrong,
yet I know that someone feels that I have
wronged them.

Help me to be both brave and kind towards
them, even though they are being angry and
spiteful.

Help me to rebuild respect and friendship
between us.

820 All Kinds of Sorry

Dear God,
For the silly things I have done wrong
I am sorry.

For the serious things I have done wrong
I am sorry.

For the things I didn't even know were wrong
I am sorry.

For all the things I need to put right
Make me strong.

Sophie Piper

821 The Trail of Destruction

Dear God,
Please forgive our mistakes:
each angry moment,
each careless word,
each trail of destruction.

822 Forgetting and Remembering

Dear God,
Help me to forget my mistakes but to
remember what they taught me.

823 Walking to Heaven

Dear God,
Please forget the bad things that I do
And forgive the good things I forget.
I'm walking each day on the road to
    your heaven
But I'm not very close to it yet.

824 Inside One's Heart

O great Chief, light a candle within my heart
that I may see what is therein and sweep the
rubbish from your dwelling place.

Prayer of an African girl

825 The Tangle of Lies

Dear God,
The lies I told have grown like brambles,
and now I am trapped in a tangle of thorns.

Dear God, I don't know what to do; I just
want to be free again to tell the truth.

826 Thief

O God,
I am a thief.
I took it.
I have it.
I might be found out.
I am more scared than sorry.
I need a way to put things right.

Wanting a New Start

827 River of Forgiveness

The things I ought not to have done,
   dear God,
I bring to the river of your forgiveness.
I throw them into the torrent of love
and wait for them to be carried far
   from sight
and from all remembering.

828 Rainbow of Forgiveness

O God,
I have done so many things wrong.
I am surrounded by dark clouds of misery.

Send me the rainbow of your forgiveness
and let me walk through its shimmering
   archway
into the clear blue day of your love.

829 God's Mercy

There's a wideness in God's mercy
Like the wideness of the sea.

F.W. Faber (1814–63)

830 Trying to Forgive Myself

O God,
I can forgive my friends quite quickly.
I can forgive my enemies eventually.
But how long will it take before I can
forgive myself?

831 Take Away My Wrongdoing

Take my wrongdoing
and throw it away,
down in the deep of the sea;
welcome me into your kingdom of love
for all of eternity.

Based on Micah 7:18–20

832 Open Our Eyes

Open our eyes, so that we may see the
colours of God's love.

Victoria Tebbs

833 Change Me

Dear God,
Please forgive the wrong things I have done.
Please accept me the way I am.
Please change me into what I should be.

834 Confession

I confess to you, O Lord,
all that I have done wrong.
Speak your forgiveness
into my heart
and help me to make
a new beginning.

835 The Deep Root of Mischief

O God,
There is some mischief in me, deep
as a dandelion root and bringing forth
a thousand little seeds of naughtiness.

Turn that mischief into kindliness to produce
a million good deeds and more.

836 When I Get Really Angry

Dear God,
When I get really angry,
I sometimes yell things I don't really mean.
Then, when I have shouted out my anger,
I find I have wounded my friends so much,
I cannot undo the damage.

Dear God,
I am truly sorry.
Heal my friends of the damage I have done.
Help me to find a better way to deal with
being angry.

837 I Told God Everything

I told God everything:
I told God about all the wrong things
  I had done.
I gave up trying to pretend.
I gave up trying to hide.
I knew that the only thing to do was
  to confess.

And God forgave me.

Based on Psalm 32:5

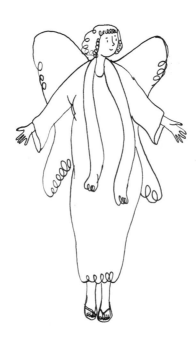

838 Be Merciful to Me

Be merciful to me, O God,
  because of your constant love.
Because of your great mercy
  wipe away my sins!

I recognize my faults;
  I am always conscious of my sins.
I have sinned against you – only against you –
  and done what you consider evil.
So you are right in judging me.

Sincerity and truth are what you require;
  fill my mind with your wisdom.

Create a pure heart in me, O God,
  and put a new and loyal spirit in me.

Give me again the joy that comes from your
    salvation,
  and make me willing to obey you.

Psalm 51:1, 3, 4, 6, 10, 12

839 Making Amends

Making amends
is an uphill road
and stony is the way.
At the top of the hill
you will find the gate
to a bright new shining day.

840 Please Stay Faithful to Me

Dear God,
If ever I fail to be faithful to you, please will
you stay faithful to me.

Based on 2 Timothy 2:13

841 Things Worth Having

O God,
Help me to see that the things worth having
cannot be won by cheating.

842 Come Back to God

Come back to the Lord your God.
  He is kind and full of mercy;
  he is patient and keeps his promise;
  he is always ready to forgive and not punish.

Joel 2:13

843 Lord Have Mercy

God above us,
God before us,
God rules.
May the King of Heaven
give now the portion of mercy.

Black Book of Carmarthen
(10th–11th centuries)

844 Have Pity!

God, have pity on me, a sinner!

From Jesus' parable of the Pharisee
and the tax collector, Luke 18:13

FORGIVING OTHERS

845 The Grudge

How to forgive:

Take one grudge
and drop it in the deep pond of forgetting.
Wait a while.

Within each ugly grudge
is the seed of forgiveness
and it will grow
into the tree of peace.

846 The Mud and the Flower

From the mud
a pure white flower

From the storm
a clear blue sky

As we pardon
one another

God forgives us
from on high.

Sophie Piper

847 Cherish Pity

Cherish pity, lest you drive an angel
from your door.

William Blake (1757–1827)

848 How Can I Forgive?

O God,
How can I forgive?
Why should I forgive?

How can I agree to be friends again?
Why should I agree to be friends again?

O God,
I know what you will say:
You will say that I can forgive because
    you can forgive.
You will say that I should forgive because
    you forgive us all.

O God,
I have no forgiveness in me.
I will have to borrow yours.

849 Not Ready

Dear God,
I am not ready to forgive
but I am ready to be made ready.

850 Too Angry

Dear God,
I know who I should be praying for, but
right now I'm so angry with them I'd rather
leave the choice of blessings – or, indeed,
punishments – up to you.

851 Really Nasty

Dear God,
I'd like something really nasty to happen to
my enemies, unless you have a better idea.

852 The Unforgiveable

O God,
How can I forgive the unforgiveable?

– Remember that my mercy is greater than
any wrong that can be done on your small
earth. But do not hurry to offer your
forgiveness. First come and sit with me,
and I will comfort you.

853 Remembering the Good Things

O Lord, remember not only the men and
women of good will, but also those of ill
will. But do not remember all the suffering
they have inflicted on us; remember the
fruits we have borne, thanks to this
suffering – our comradeship, our loyalty,
our courage, our generosity, the greatness
of heart which has grown out of all this,
and when they come to judgment let all
the fruits which we have borne be their
forgiveness.

Prayer written by an unknown prisoner
in Ravensbruck concentration camp and
left by the body of a dead child

854 Delivering an Apology

Dear God,
What can I do when an apology is flung
back at me?

I can pick it up gently and take it to the
gates of heaven, and ask an angel to deliver
it for me.

855 The Forgiveness Between Us

O God,
Be the forgiveness between us when we
cannot forgive one another.

856 Take Me By the Hand

Dear Jesus,
I find it hard to love my enemies.
I do not want to pray for those who are
cruel to me.

I want to follow you, but you are walking
far ahead of me.
Please come and take me by the hand.

Based on Matthew 5:43–48

20 Praying with the Bible

857 Understanding the Bible

Dear God,
Help me when I read the Bible.

Sometimes it is hard to understand the
words; sometimes I understand the words
but I am still puzzled about what they are
trying to say.

Help me to learn what is the good and
right way to live.

Based on 2 Timothy 3:16

LEARNING FROM BIBLE STORIES

858 Praise to the Creator God

Praise be to God on Mondays:
to the God who made day and night.

Praise be to God on Tuesdays:
to the God who made heaven and earth.

Praise be to God on Wednesdays:
to the God who made sea and land,
trees and grasses, flowers and fruit.

Praise be to God on Thursdays:
to the God who made sun and moon,
and the stars that whirl through the universe.

Praise be to God on Fridays:
to the God who made fish to fill the deep
   of the seas
and birds to fly high in the heavens.

Praise be to God on Saturdays:
to the God who made every kind of creature –
the great and the small, the wild and the tame;
to the God who made men and women,
girls and boys, guardians of the wide earth.

Praise be to God on Sundays:
to the God who made a day of thankfulness,
a day of rest.

Based on Genesis 1

859 Keep Us Safe

God of Noah,
who sent the flood,
may the earth be clean of wickedness.

God of Noah,
who sent the rainbow,
do not destroy your people.

God of Noah,
keep us safe in the ark of your love,
and may we have faith to keep us from
sinking in despair.

Inspired by Genesis 7–8

860 I Put My Trust in You

O God,
Be a friend to me
as you were to Abraham in days of old:
for in spite of my many mistakes
I put my trust in you.

Based on Genesis 15:6

861 Family Quarrels

Dear God,
Joseph's family was not a happy one, but
you brought good out of something bad.

You kept Joseph safe when his brothers
    sold him as a slave.
You made him wise so that he was given
    power in Egypt.
You helped him to forgive his family when
    they came begging.
Through Joseph, you saved the whole family.

Help everyone whose family quarrels.
Bring good out of their bad situation.

Inspired by the story of Joseph, Genesis 37–47

862 Make a Way for Us

Dear God,
You made a path for Moses and the people
of Israel.

When they thought there was no way
forward and no way back, you made a way
through the sea and kept them safe.

Make a way for us when we are in trouble
and afraid, and bring us safely home.

Inspired by the escape of the Israelites, Exodus 14

863 Let Us Listen

Father God,
who spoke to the boy Samuel in the temple,
let us listen for your voice calling,
and let us be ready to serve you.

864 In Difficult Situations

Dear God,
When we face situations that are too difficult
for us, may we remember the story of David
and Goliath, and trust that you will help us.

865 Standing Up to Wickedness

Almighty God,
Help us learn from the story of Elijah to
be faithful to you when the world seems
to be a wicked place.

May we stand up to wickedness.

May we listen for your still, small voice
of calm in the midst of danger.

866 Protect and Bless Us

Dear God,
Like Daniel who faced the lions, may we
be true to you even when people mock us
and hate us because we pray to you. May
we continue to trust in you and to do good.
Protect us from danger and bless us.

867 Forgiveness

We remember the story of Jonah, and of
the people of Nineveh who were famous
for their wickedness. We remember that
Jonah found it hard to tell the Ninevites
that you were ready to forgive them.

We, too, find it hard to accept that you will forgive wicked people. Then we remember our own failings, and are glad that you are ready to forgive us and all people.

868 Listening and Serving

Dear Jesus,
Make me more like Martha: eager to serve
  you.
Make me more like Mary: eager to listen
  to your teaching.

869 Lift Us Up

Lord Jesus,
In times of danger our faith sometimes fails, and we sink, like Peter trying to walk on water. Lift us up, give us new courage, and bring us to safety.

870 Prayer of the Lost Sheep

Dear God,
I am your lost sheep.
Please find me.
Please take me home.

871 Giving You Thanks

Kind Jesus,
You healed ten lepers, but only one returned
to thank you. Help us to notice the many
ways in which you bless us, and make us
ready to give you thanks.

872 The Cockerel

Dear God,
This night has been darker than any other
I have known, but now I stand on the brink
of dawn. I do not know what the day will
bring.

I only know that light is stronger than the
darkness, so I will crow and crow; yes, I
will crow to divide that which belongs to
darkness from that which belongs to the
light.

873 Caring for One Another

Lord Jesus,
As you asked your disciple John to take care
of your mother, Mary, help all of us who
follow you to care for one another as family.

874 Waiting for God

Lord Jesus,
As Mary Magdalen wept at your crucifixion,
so do we.

As Mary Magdalen waited for good news,
so do we.

As Mary Magdalen saw you in the Easter
garden, so we long to you see you face to
face.

875 Change Our Minds and Hearts

Dear God,
Thank you for the example of Paul. Thank
you that you speak to us even when we
have no faith in Jesus. Thank you that you
can change our minds and our hearts, and
make us useful in your service.

876 Growing in Faith

Dear God,
As the boy Timothy learned from his mother
and grandmother to believe in Jesus, may we
be eager and willing to learn from the faith
of our parents and grandparents.

21 Christian Festivals and Celebrations

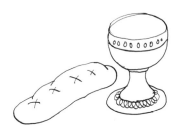

877 The Christian Year

Harvest time is gold and red:
Thank God for our daily bread.
Christmas time is red and green:
Heaven now on earth is seen.
Easter time is green and white:
Bring us all to heaven's light.
Pentecost is white and gold:
God's own spirit makes us bold.

878 Heaven in Our Lives

Christmas is the time when angels open
the gates from heaven to earth:
let us welcome heaven into our lives.

Easter is the time when angels open
the gates from earth to heaven:
let us follow Jesus into God's kingdom.

ADVENT

879 Advent Prayer

Dear God,
Be the flame to light my way through the
dark times, when I sit and wait for Jesus to
come near.

Dear God,
Be the flame to warm my soul through the
cold times, when I sit and wait for Jesus to
come near.

Dear God,
Be the flame to cheer my heart through the
sad times, when I sit and wait for Jesus to
come near.

Dear God,
Be the flame to spark and sing through the
silent times, when I sit and wait for Jesus to
come near.

Dear God,
May Jesus be with me this day and every day:
my light and my salvation.

880 Come, Jesus!

Come, thou long-expected Jesus,
   Born to set thy people free,
From our fears and sins release us,
   Let us find our rest in thee.

Charles Wesley (1707–88)

881 Thoughts Before Christmas

"Don't be thinking Christmas yet –
we haven't reached December."
Well, that's what people tell me.
But why? Don't they remember
two thousand years have passed
since Jesus came down to this earth?
So I shall give my whole life long
to celebrate his birth.

882 Saint Nicholas

Dear God,
Thank you for the story of Saint Nicholas,
who brought gifts to rescue a family from
poverty and unhappiness. May our Christmas
gifts bring help and joy to everyone, and may
we be rich in faith and love.

883 I Count the Days to Christmas

I count the days to Christmas
and I watch the evening sky.
I want to see the angels
as to Bethlehem they fly.

I'm watching for the wise men
and the royal shining star.
Please may I travel with them?
Is the stable very far?

I count the days to Christmas
as we shop and bake and clean.
The lights and tinsel sparkle,
and yet deep inside I dream

that as we tell the story
of Lord Jesus and his birth,
the things of every day will fade
as heaven comes to earth.

CHRISTMAS

884 A Christmas Blessing

Let us remember Mary this Christmas
And may God bless our mothers.

Let us remember Joseph this Christmas
And may God bless our fathers.

Let us remember Elizabeth and Zechariah
   and John this Christmas
And may God bless all our relatives.

Let us remember the shepherds this Christmas
And may God bless all those who will be
   working.

Let us remember the wise men this Christmas
And may God bless all those who will be
   travelling.

Let us remember Jesus this Christmas
And may God bless us all and make us his
   children.

885 Blessing the Crib

We have made a manger
lined with softest hay;
Jesus, please be with us
all through Christmas Day.

886 Let Us Travel to Christmas

Let us travel to Christmas
By the light of a star.
Let us go to the hillside
Right where the shepherds are.
Let us see shining angels
Singing from heaven above.
Let us see Mary cradling
God's holy child with love.

887 Away in a Manger

Away in a manger, no crib for a bed,
The little Lord Jesus laid down his sweet head.
The stars in the bright sky looked down where
  he lay,
The little Lord Jesus asleep on the hay.

The cattle are lowing, the baby awakes,
But little Lord Jesus no crying he makes.
I love thee, Lord Jesus! Look down from the
  sky,
And stay by my side until morning is nigh.

Be near me, Lord Jesus; I ask thee to stay
Close by me for ever, and love me, I pray.
Bless all the dear children in thy tender care,
And fit us for heaven, to live with thee there.

Traditional

888 Rejoice and Be Merry

Rejoice and be merry in songs and in mirth!
O praise our Redeemer, all mortals on earth!
For this is the birthday of Jesus our King,
Who brought us salvation – his praises we'll
   sing!

A heavenly vision appeared in the sky.
Vast numbers of angels the shepherds did spy,
Proclaiming the birthday of Jesus our King,
Who brought us salvation – his praises we'll
   sing!

Likewise a bright star in the sky did appear,
Which led the Wise Men from the east to
   draw near:
They found the Messiah, sweet Jesus our King,
Who brought us salvation – his praises we'll
   sing!

And when they were come, they their
    treasure unfold,
And unto him offered myrrh, incense
    and gold:
So blessed for ever be Jesus our King,
Who brought us salvation – his praises
    we'll sing!

Anonymous

889 The Christmas News

Angels sang the Christmas news
To shepherds by their fold:
As we share
With love and care
The message still is told.

890 Love at Christmas

God, our loving Father, help us remember
the birth of Jesus, that we may share in
the song of the angels, the gladness of the
shepherds and the wisdom of the wise men.

Close the door of hate and open the door
of love all over the world.

Let kindness come with every gift and good
desires with every greeting.

Deliver us from evil by the blessing which
Christ brings and teach us to be merry with
clean hearts.

May the Christmas morning make us happy
to be your children and the Christmas
evening bring us to our beds with grateful
thoughts, forgiving and forgiven, for Jesus'
sake. Amen.

Robert Louis Stevenson (1850–94)

891 The Stars that Shine at Christmas

The stars that shine at Christmas
Shine on throughout the year;
Jesus, born so long ago,
Still gathers with us here.
We listen to his stories,
We learn to say his prayer,
We follow in his footsteps
And learn to love and share.

892 Love Came Down at Christmas

Love came down at Christmas,
Love all lovely, Love Divine;
Love was born at Christmas,
Star and Angels gave the sign.

Christina Rossetti (1830–94)

893 Bombs at Christmas

This Christmas there will be lights in the sky
and shepherds will cower in fear
when they see the anti-aircraft fire
and know enemy planes are near.

The light and the fire will tell out the news
of ill will and war on earth
and bombs will rain down near the humble
  room
where a mother has just given birth.

And so, let us pray for a miracle
of one holy, silent night
and ask God to give us the wisdom we need
to help put the world to right.

894 What Can I Give Him?

What can I give him,
Poor as I am?
If I were a shepherd
I would bring a lamb;
If I were a wise man
I would do my part;
Yet what I can I give him –
Give my heart.

Christina Rossetti (1830–94)

EPIPHANY

895 Gifts at Christmas

Lord Jesus,
The wise men brought you gold:
Let us use our riches to do good.

The wise men brought you frankincense:
Let our prayers rise like smoke to heaven.

The wise men brought you myrrh:
Let us seek to comfort those who are sad
    and grieving.

Lord Jesus,
You have given us so many rich gifts:
Let us use them to do your work in this
    world.

896 Lead Us Also

Dear God,
As you led the wise men,
may you also lead us –
to the court of heaven,
to the prince of peace,
to the king of love.

897 The Wise Men's Story

The wise men read the skies above,
and now we read their story
of how they found the prince of peace,
newborn from heaven's glory.

We come, as if to Bethlehem,
to offer gifts of love
to make this world at Christmas time
a piece of heaven above.

CANDLEMAS

898 For Candlemas

Candle, burn with golden fire
in the darkest night;
Jesus, help me follow you;
make my whole world bright.

899 Light of the World

Jesus, you are the light of the world.
May we live our lives as you taught, so
that your light will shine through us in
all we think and say and do.

THE SEASON OF LENT

900 Ash Wednesday

Fire so golden, ash so grey,
Now we come to God and pray;

Fire so lively, ash so dead,
Our confession must be said;

Heaven's wind, blow ash away,
Round God's fire let us stay.

901 Lent

Lent is a time
for giving up something valuable
so we can remember
how great a blessing it is.

Lent is a time
for taking up something valuable
so we can remember
to bring some blessing to others.

902 Mothering Sunday

We, who are mothers,
pray for our children
and all the children in the world.

We, who have mothers,
pray for our mothers
and all the mothers in the world.

903 Mother's Day

As Mary cradled the infant Jesus
so mothers cradle their babies.

As Mary worried about her missing son
so mothers worry about their children.

As Mary believed her son could work miracles
so mothers believe in their children's talents.

As Mary wept at Jesus' crucifixion
so mothers weep at their children's suffering.

God, who blessed Mary,
bless all mothers with the strength to go
on loving and to trust that God will make all
the things that happen to their children work
together for the good.

HOLY WEEK

904 Palm Sunday

We sing and clap and wave and cheer
for Jesus, who comes riding near.

We cheer and wave and clap and sing
to welcome Jesus as our king.

905 Jesus is Our King

Let us welcome Jesus as our king:

King of peace,
King of love,
King in death,
King of life.

906 **Maundy Thursday**

Kind Jesus,
Welcome us to the room you have made
    ready.
Wash us clean from the dust of the journey.
Bless us as we share the bread and wine.

907 **Last Supper**

Jesus' body,
Broken bread,
By God's word
We all are fed.

Jesus' lifeblood,
Wine that's spilt,
As one temple
We are built.

At this table
Take your place:
Feast upon
God's love and grace.

908 Maundy Night

Let us not fall asleep:
let us keep watch with Jesus.

Let us not fall asleep:
let us pray that we will be kept from
  hard testing.

Let us not fall asleep:
let us keep faith with those who are
  suffering now.

Let us not fall asleep:
let us keep watch with Jesus.

909 Jesus' Selflessness

It is a thing most wonderful,
almost too wonderful to be,
that God's own Son should come from
  heaven,
and die to save a child like me.

And yet I know that it is true:
he chose a poor and humble lot,
and wept and toiled and mourned and died
for love of those who loved him not.

William Walsham How (1823–97)

910 I Will Walk with Jesus

I will walk with Jesus.
– But you may be betrayed.
I will walk with Jesus.
– But you may be abandoned.
I will walk with Jesus.
– But you may be given a cross too heavy
  to bear.
I will walk with Jesus.
– But you cannot know where that may lead.
I will walk with Jesus.
– Then may Jesus walk with you through
  life and through death.

911 There is a Green Hill

There is a green hill far away,
  Without a city wall,
Where the dear Lord was crucified
  Who died to save us all.

We may not know, we cannot tell,
  What pains he had to bear,
But we believe it was for us
  He hung and suffered there.

He died that we might be forgiven,
  He died to make us good;
That we might go at last to heaven,
  Saved by his Precious Blood.

There was no other good enough
   To pay the price of sin;
He only could unlock the gate
   Of heaven, and let us in.

O, dearly, dearly has he loved,
   And we must love him too,
And trust in his redeeming Blood,
   And try his works to do.

Cecil Frances Alexander (1818–95)

EASTER

912 Good Friday and Easter

The winter branches were bare and grey
But now the blossom is white,
And Christ was hung on a tree to die
But God has put all things right.

913 Roll Away the Stone of Death

Come, Holy Angels,
into this dark night.
Roll away the stone of death.
Let the light of life
shine from heaven.

914 Death is Put Away

The tree of thorns
is dressed in white
for resurrection day;
and joy springs from
the underworld
now death is put away.

915 Rejoice at Easter

Christ is now risen again
From all his death and all his pain:
Therefore will we merry be,
And rejoice with him gladly. *Kyrieleison.**

Had he not risen again,
We had been lost, this is plain:
But since he is risen in deed,
Let us love him all with speed. *Kyrieleison.*

Now is a time of gladness,
To sing of the Lord's goodness:
Therefore glad now we will be,
And rejoice in him only. *Kyrieleison.*

Miles Coverdale (1488–1568)

** Kyrieleison (usually Kyrie eleison) is
Greek for the prayer "Lord, have mercy".*

916 Easter Joy

Good Friday is locked in winter,
in grief and death and dark;
Easter Sunday begins the springtime,
rising up like the lark.

917 Rejoice at Easter

The whole bright world rejoices now:
with laughing cheer! with boundless joy!
The birds do sing on every bough:
Alleluia!

Then shout beneath the racing skies:
with laughing cheer! with boundless joy!
To him who rose that we might rise:
Alleluia!

God, Father, Son and Holy Ghost:
with laughing cheer! with boundless joy!
Our God most high, our joy, our boast:
Alleluia!

Easter carol (17th century)

918 Death is Not the End

The autumn leaves were laid to rest
But now the trees are green,
And signs that God brings all to life
Throughout the world are seen.

And Jesus is alive, they say,
And death is not the end.
We rise again in heaven's light
With Jesus as our friend.

919 Lord Jesus, Who Rose Again

Lord Jesus, who died upon the cross:
You know this world's suffering,
You know this world's sorrowing,
You know this world's dying.

In your name, Lord Jesus, who rose again:
I will work for this world's healing,
I will work for this world's rejoicing,
I will work for this world's living.

920 In the Easter Garden

In the Easter garden
the leaves are turning green;
in the Easter garden
the risen Lord is seen.

In the Easter garden
we know that God above
brings us all to heaven
through Jesus and his love.

921 Life Comes Leaping

Winter death
and springtime breath;
winter grief
and springtime leaf;
winter sleep
but life comes leaping
from the darkest deep.

922 Easter is About...

Good Friday is about
burdens loaded on innocent shoulders
and nails hammered into innocent hands,
a spear piercing an innocent heart
and death enshrouding an innocent life.

Easter is about
unexpected and joyful reunions
and simple meals shared with friends,
old grievances forgiven and forgotten
and angels rolling wide the way to heaven.

923 Easter Sunrise

Friday sunset, black and red.
Weep, for Jesus Christ is dead.

Sunday sunrise, white and gold.
Christ is risen, as foretold.

924 Thomas' Easter

We celebrate Easter with the disciples who
saw the risen Jesus,
and who knew that love was stronger than
death.

We also remember Thomas, for whom
Easter was a long time coming,
and all those who feel alone in their doubt
and despair this Easter.

Risen Jesus, make yourself known to us
all in due time
so we may know for sure the joy of heaven.

ASCENSION, PENTECOST AND TRINITY

925 A Prayer for Ascension Day

Christ has no body now on earth but yours,
no hands but yours, no feet but yours...
Yours are the feet with which he is to go
    about doing good,
and yours are the hands with which he is
    to bless us now.

St Teresa of Avila (1515–82)

926 Let the Spirit Come

Let the Spirit come
like the winds that blow:
take away my doubts;
help my faith to grow.

Let the Spirit come
like a flame of gold:
warm my soul within;
make me strong and bold.

927 Wind and Fire

Let the wind of the Spirit blow from heaven
Let the fire of the Spirit glow from heaven.

Let the wind of the Spirit shake our lives
Let the fire of the Spirit shape our lives.

928 Be Close to Me

Holy Spirit of God,
be close to me
in the rushing wind,
and make me bold to do good.
Be close to me
in the golden fire
and help me do deeds
of shining goodness.

Sophie Piper

929 Glory to the Trinity

O Father, my hope:
O Son, my refuge:
O Holy Spirit, my protection:
Holy Trinity, glory to thee.

St Ioannikos

930 All Glory to God

All glory to the Father,
All glory to the Son,
All glory to the Spirit:
God in three, yet one.

Victoria Tebbs

MICHAELMAS AND HALLOWTIDE

931 The Archangel Michael

As Michael and all the angels
threw the dragon of evil from heaven,
so may I fight evil in this world
with the help of God's holy angels.

932 A Psalm for Hallowe'en

I sing a song of praise to God
throughout the darkest night,
for guarding me, for guiding me
to know what's good and right.
No evil things will frighten me,
no shadows from the tomb,
for God is light and life and power
to scatter midnight's gloom.

Based on Psalm 16:7–11

933 A Prayer at Hallowe'en

Guard us through the night, dear God,
and keep us safe from harm;
from all our wild imaginings
and every false alarm.

934 People Who Follow Jesus

Dear God,
We think of the people
we know today
who help us
to follow Jesus.

We think of the people
from days gone by
whose stories help us
to follow Jesus.

We think of their wise words
and their good deeds
and ask you to help us
to follow Jesus.

935 Learning from the Saints

Dear God,
Thank you for the example of other
Christians. From the stories of their faith,
may I grow in understanding. From the
stories of their kind-hearted deeds, may
I learn to do good.

936 All Souls

Let us remember before God all those
  who have died:
whose bodies now belong to the good earth;
whose souls are safe in God's eternal love
as we also are safe in God's eternal love.

937 Darkness is Falling

Darkness is falling.
Dear God, give us your true light.

Darkness is falling.
Dear God, give us your true life.

Darkness is falling.
Dear God, give us your true love.

938 On All Souls' Day

On All Souls' Day
we look to the earth
where loved ones were laid
to rest.

On All Souls' Day
we look to heaven
where loved ones by God
are blessed.

CHURCH SERVICES AND CELEBRATIONS

939 A Family Service

We have come together, dear God,
    to worship you:
mums and dads, sons and daughters,
aunts and uncles, nieces and nephews
    and cousins,
grandparents and children.

We have come together, dear God,
    to worship you
because we are your children
and we want to live as your family.

940 An Evening Service

At the ending of the day
we gather together
and remember God's blessings.

At the ending of the day
we gather together
and remember God's love.

At the ending of the day
we gather together
and ask for God's peace in our hearts.

941 Sunday Prayer

Help me, Lord,
to be quiet and still,
to hear your voice,
to know your will.

Help me, Lord,
to sing loud and clear,
to praise your name
through all the year.

942 Day of Rest

Thank you, kind God, for your day of
rest. May we spend its hours on things
that bring us joy.

943 For the Choir

Let us sing to God
In the harmony of voices.

Let us sing to God
In the harmony of love.

Let us sing to God
In giving and forgiving.

Let our praises ring
From earth to heaven above.

944 A Wedding Prayer

Bless the dress
and bless the flowers
and bless the wedding weather;
bless the couple,
bless the life
that they will live together.

945 Love and Marriage

Dear God,
Thank you for this special day.
Thank you for the love we feel all around us.

Olwen Turchetta

946 For Wedding Attendants

Dear God, we are waiting here, ready for the
   wedding.
May the bride and groom be pleased with
   how we look.
May the bride and groom be pleased with
   what we do.
May all the wedding be lovely for them,
and may their marriage be full of happiness.

947 A Christening Prayer

We gather round
to welcome baby
into God's family.

We will love you
and help you to grow up good.

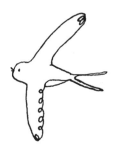

948 A Confirmation Prayer

When I was a child,
others made promises
that I should be brought up
to know you.
Now I am older
I want to say yes,
I am glad they did this
and that you are my friend.
Yet, I am still your child
and I want to continue
following you, Lord Jesus,
and loving you more each day.

Su Box

949 On My Confirmation

Grant us, Lord, to continue as we have
begun, with faith, prayer and the strength
of your Holy Spirit. Through good and bad
times, through joy and sorrow, through
success and setbacks, help us to hold fast
to the faith we have professed, knowing
that you, who have called us, are faithful,
trustworthy and true.

Rebecca Winter

950 A Confirmation Blessing

Go, and know that the Lord goes with you:
let God lead you each day
into the quiet place of your heart,
where he will speak with you;
know that he loves you and watches over you –
that he listens to you in gentle understanding,
that he is with you always,
wherever you are and however you may feel:
and the blessings of God – Father, Son
and Holy Spirit – be yours for ever.

Rebecca Winter

22 Night-time Blessings

951 Day is Done

Day is done,
Gone the sun
From the lake,
From the hills,
From the sky.
Safely rest,
All is well!
God is nigh.

Anonymous

THANKS FOR THE DAY

952 For Another Day

Thank you, God in heaven,
For a day begun.
Thank you for the breezes,
Thank you for the sun.
For this time of gladness,
For our work and play,
Thank you, God in heaven,
For another day.

Traditional

953 For the Day Just Gone

Thank you, dear God, for the day just gone.
I wasn't happy all the way through:
there was a time when it seemed that all my
    plans were ruined.
Then, out of the very thing that went wrong,
came the best thing of all.
Now I know for sure
that you blessed me.

954 Reflections

Is it so small a thing
To have enjoy'd the sun,
To have liv'd light in the spring,
To have lov'd, to have thought, to have done?

Matthew Arnold (1822–88)

955 Too Tired

Almost too tired to go to bed
Almost too tired to pray
Almost too tired to thank the Lord
For this wonderful day.

PEACE AT NIGHT

956 In the Quiet Night

In the quiet night,
I can hear the wind
that blows from heaven,
bringing life and hope
to all the earth.

957 Night Vision

Open my eyes, dear God,
To the beauty of the night:
To a world of shape and silhouette,
And scatterings of silver.

958 Let Me Drift Away

Cradle me, kind angels, in a coracle of
   darkness
Float me on the starry silver sea
Let me drift away through the waves of
   cloud and grey
To the land where morning waits for me.

959 Thank You for a Night of Rest

My Father, for another night
Of quiet sleep and rest,
For all the joy of morning light,
Your holy name be blest.

Henry William Baker (1821–77)

960 A Dark Room at Midnight

My room is dark
in deepest night:
O fill my life
with heaven's light.

I am awake
to unknown fear:
O send the angels
very near.

Then let me
softly fall asleep
till sunbeams
through the window creep.

961 Worries

Worries come in the night
like chilling rain.
They spatter against the window
and on the roof;
but I am safe in God's shelter,
in a tent of holy dreams.
Nothing will dampen my spirits,
nothing will chill my soul.

962 Awake and Afraid

O God,
I am awake in the night and afraid:
afraid because I cannot see clearly
but instead imagine all manner of things.

O God,
Turn my mind to pleasant imaginings
and turn my imaginings to happy dreams
and turn my happy dreams to quiet sleep
   again.

963 Ghoulies and Ghosties

From ghoulies and ghosties
Long-leggety beasties
And things that go bump in the night,
Good Lord deliver us.

Traditional Cornish prayer

964 Dreaming of Dreaming

My bed is like a boat,
but where will I sail tonight?

On the rough sea of wakefulness.
Oh, please not!

On the swirling torrent of nightmares.
No, not that.

On the calm lake of sleep.
Yes, that's better.

And down the sunlit river of dreams.
Already I'm dreaming of dreaming.

965 Hold Us by the Hand

Lord, when we have not any light,
And mothers are asleep,
Then through the stillness of the night
Thy little children keep.

When shadows haunt the quiet room,
Help us to understand
That thou art with us through the gloom,
To hold us by the hand.

Annie Matheson (1853–1924)

966 A Great Relief

The day God gave is over
and that's a great relief,
because right from this morning
it only brought me grief.

967 By the Light of God

Walking in the light of the sun
Walking by the light of God.

Walking in the light of the moon
Walking by the light of God.

Walking in the dark of the night
Walking by the light of God.

968 The Heavenly Sea

The moon is afloat on the heavenly sea
And I wait on dreamland's shore;
Dear God, let me sleep
Through the dark so deep
Until the night is no more.

969 The Moon Shines Bright

The moon shines bright,
The stars give light
Before the break of day;
God bless you all
Both great and small
And send a joyful day.

Traditional

970 Matthew, Mark, Luke and John

Matthew, Mark, Luke and John,
Bless the bed that I lie on.
Before I lay me down to sleep,
I pray the Lord my soul to keep.
Four corners to my bed,
Four angels there are spread,
Two at the foot, two at the head:
Four to carry me when I'm dead.
I go by sea, I go by land,
The Lord made me with his right hand.
Should any danger come to me,
Sweet Jesus Christ deliver me.
He's the branch and I'm the flower,
Pray God send me a happy hour,
And should I die before I wake,
I pray the Lord my soul to take.

Traditional

971 Evening Time

Now is the evening time
when angels wrap the earth
in a dark and downy quilt.

Now is the evening time
when angels wrap the world
in a deep and dreamy sleep.

Now is the evening time
when angels watch the world
by the light of a million stars.

972 Let Me Sleep

Let me sleep
in a corner of darkness

Let me sleep
in a corner of softness

Let me sleep
in a corner of kindness

Let me sleep
in a corner of blessedness.

973 Quiet Sleep

Now the daylight goes away,
Saviour listen while I pray,
Asking thee to watch and keep
And to send me quiet sleep.

Jesus, Saviour, wash away
All that has been wrong today.
Help me every day to be
Good and gentle, more like thee.

Revd W.H. Havergal (1793–1870)

974 Peace of the Running Waves

Deep peace of the running waves to you,
Deep peace of the flowing air to you,
Deep peace of the quiet earth to you,
Deep peace of the shining stars to you,
Deep peace of the shades of night to you,
Moon and stars always giving light to you,
Deep peace of Christ, the Son of Peace,
    to you.

Traditional Gaelic blessing

975 Peace in My Heart

Send your peace into my heart, O Lord,
that I may be contented
with your mercies of this day and confident
of your protection for this night;
and having forgiven others,
even as you forgive me,
may I go to my rest in peaceful trust
through Jesus Christ, our Lord, Amen.

St Francis of Assisi (1181–1226)

976 Others Are Crying

The night-time world around me is quiet;
but in this same darkness others are crying.

Some are grieving,
some are hurting,
some are in danger.

O God,
bring them comfort,
bring them healing,
bring them safety.

977 An Evening Prayer

An evening prayer
as the sun sinks low:
we thank you, God,
for this world below.

An evening prayer
as the dark comes nigh:
we thank you, God,
for your heaven on high.

GOD WATCH OVER ME

978 Dreamland's Drifting Sea

God of quiet nights of sleep
Float me on the darkness deep
Out on dreamland's drifting sea
With an angel guarding me.

979 Guard Me

The night is come, like to the day;
Depart not thou, great God, away…
Guard me 'gainst those watchful foes,
Whose eyes are open while mine close.

Sir Thomas Browne (1605–82))

980 All Through the Night

Sleep, my child, and peace attend thee,
All through the night;
Guardian angels God will send thee,
All through the night.
Soft the drowsy hours are creeping,
Hill and vale in slumber sleeping,
I my loving vigil keeping,
All through the night.

Traditional Welsh prayer

981 Bless Me and My Friends

Jesus, tender Shepherd, hear me,
Bless your little lamb tonight;
Through the darkness please be near me;
Keep me safe till morning light.

All this day your hand has led me,
And I thank you for your care;
You have warmed and clothed and fed me;
Listen to my evening prayer.

Let my sins be all forgiven,
Bless the friends I love so well;
Take me, when I die, to heaven,
Happy there with you to dwell.

Mary Lundie Duncan (1814–40)

982 Evening (in Words of One Syllable)

The day is past, the sun is set,
  And the white stars are in the sky;
While the long grass with dew is wet,
  And through the air the bats now fly.

The lambs have now lain down to sleep,
  The birds have long since sought their nests;
The air is still; and dark, and deep
  On the hill side the old wood rests.

Yet of the dark I have no fear,
  But feel as safe as when 'tis light;
For I know God is with me there,
  And He will guard me through the night.

For God is by me when I pray,
   And when I close mine eyes in sleep,
I know that He will with me stay,
   And will all night watch by me keep.

For He who rules the stars and sea,
   Who makes the grass and trees to grow,
Will look on a poor child like me,
   When on my knees I to Him bow.

He holds all things in His right hand,
   The rich, the poor, the great, the small;
When we sleep, or sit, or stand,
   Is with us, for He loves us all.

Thomas Miller (1807–74)

983 Now the Day is Over

Now the day is over,
  Night is drawing nigh.
Shadows of the evening
  Steal across the sky.

Now the darkness gathers,
  Stars begin to peep,
Birds and beasts and flowers
  Soon will be asleep.

Jesu, give the weary
  Calm and sweet repose;
With thy tenderest blessing
  May our eyelids close.

Through the long night-watches
  May thine Angels spread
Their white wings above me,
  Watching round my bed.

When the morning wakens,
  Then may I arise,
Pure, and fresh, and sinless
  In thy holy eyes.

Glory to the Father,
Glory to the Son,
And to thee, blest Spirit
Whilst all ages run.

Sabine Baring-Gould (1834–1924)

984 Glory to Thee, My God, this Night

Glory to thee, my God, this night,
For all the blessings of the light;
Keep me, O keep me, King of kings,
Beneath thine everlasting wings.

Praise God from whom all blessings flow;
Praise him, all creatures here below;
Praise him above, ye heavenly host;
Praise Father, Son, and Holy Ghost.

Bishop Thomas Ken (1637–1711)

985 Keep Us Safe this Night

Lord, keep us safe this night,
Secure from all our fears;
May angels guard us while we sleep,
Till morning light appears.

John Leland (1754–1841)

986 Angels Watching

Clouds in the sky above,
Waves on the sea,
Angels up in heaven
Watching over you and me.

Christina Goodings

987 Heavenly Blessings

Hush! my dear, lie still and slumber,
Holy angels guard thy bed!
Heavenly blessings without number
Gently falling on thy head.

Isaac Watts (1674–1748)

988 Ocean of Night

The ocean of night is rolling in
over the heavens of blue,
but angels are watching both night and day
and they will take care of you.

989 Sleep

O God,
Give us strength for the daytime
and sleep in the night-time.

990 I Lie Down

I lie down
and my home
is the shelter
of God's guarding.

I lie down
and my bed
is the comfort
of God's loving.

I lie down
and my sleep
is the peace
of God's good keeping.

991 Walk with Me

Walk with me in golden sun
Walk with me in rain
Walk with me in happiness
Walk with me in pain.

Walk with me at morning time
When the world is light
Walk with me when evening comes
Watch me through the night.

992 Guard Me Through the Night

Now I lay me down to sleep,
I pray thee, Lord, thy child to keep;
Thy love to guard me through the night
And wake me in the morning light.

Traditional

993 Bring Us Home

In the grey time of the evening
In the grey time of the year
May God bring us home in safety
May God keep us without fear.

994 Be Thou a Bright Flame

Be thou a bright flame before me,
Be thou a guiding star above me,
Be thou a smooth path below me,
And be a kindly shepherd behind me,
Today, tonight, and for ever.

I am tired and I a stranger,
Lead thou me to the land of angels;
For me it is time to go home
To the court of Christ, to the peace of heaven.

From Carmina Gadelica

995 God Protects Me

I call to God for help
and God answers me.

I lie down to sleep
and God protects me.

From Psalm 3

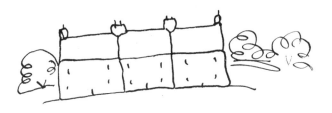

996 Sleep in Peace

When I lie down, I go to sleep in peace;
you alone, O Lord, keep me perfectly safe.

Psalm 4:8

997 Keep Us Safe

Loving Shepherd of Thy sheep,
　Keep Thy lambs, in safety keep;
Nothing can Thy power withstand;
　None can pluck us from Thy hand.

Jane Eliza Leeson (1807–82)

998 Night Peace

In the day
may I be alert to do good.

In the night
may I sleep in peace.

GOD'S BLESSING

999 May the Grace of God Rest on Us

May the grace of Christ our Saviour,
And the Father's boundless love,
With the Holy Spirit's favour,
Rest upon us from above.

John Newton (1725–1807)

1000 A Blessing for Everyone

May the grace of the Lord Jesus
be with everyone.

Revelation 22:21,
the last line of the Bible

Acknowledgments

All unattributed prayers by Lois Rock are copyright © Lion Hudson. Prayers by Su Box, Jenni Dutton, Christina Goodings, Caroline Knight, Sophie Piper, Mark Robinson, Victoria Tebbs, Olwen Turchetta and Rebecca Winter are copyright © Lion Hudson.

Bible extracts are taken or adapted from the Good News Bible, published by The Bible Societies/HarperCollins Publishers Ltd, UK © American Bible Society 1966, 1971, 1976, 1992, used with permission.

The Lord's Prayer (on page 397) from *Common Worship: Services and Prayers for the Church of England* (Church House Publishing, 2000) is copyright © The English Language Liturgical Consultation, 1988 and is reproduced by permission of the publishers.

Prayer by Mother Teresa used by permission.

Prayers from the Bible

Please note that the number after each entry is the prayer number.

Genesis 1   858
Genesis 7–8   859
Genesis 15:6   860
Genesis 26   657
Genesis 37–47   861

Exodus 14   862
Exodus 20   782
Exodus 33   783

Numbers 6:24–26   330

1 Kings 8:57–58   789

Job   666

Psalm 1   755
Psalm 3   995
Psalm 4:8   996
Psalm 5   2
Psalm 6   383
Psalm 8:1, 3–4   706
Psalm 11   684
Psalm 15   756
Psalm 16   687
Psalm 16:7–11   932
Psalm 18   688
Psalm 19   471
Psalm 22:1, 9–11, 19   384
Psalm 23   385
Psalm 23   386
Psalm 27   689
Psalm 27:1   387
Psalm 32:5   837
Psalm 34:11–14   757

Psalm 36   691
Psalm 37:3   758
Psalm 42:11 and 43:5   388
Psalm 46:1–3   389
Psalm 51:1, 3, 4, 6, 10, 12   838
Psalm 65   510
Psalm 69   390
Psalm 98   708
Psalm 103:1–4   715
Psalm 115:1   712
Psalm 119:44   759
Psalm 119:105   760
Psalm 131:1–2   391
Psalm 136:1, 4–6, 23–26   710
Psalm 148   714
Psalm 150   270
Psalm 150   716

Proverbs   787
Proverbs 8:12   784
Proverbs 10:7   785
Proverbs 10:32   786
Proverbs 20:11   788

Hosea 11:1–9   392
Hosea 14:4–8   393

Joel 2:13   842

Amos 9   664

Jonah 2   394

Micah 4:3–5   645
Micah 6:8   761

Index of Authors

Please note that the number after each entry is the prayer number.

Prayers Through the Year

Here are some suggestions for how to link the contents
of this book to themes and festivals through the months
of the year.

The number after each entry refers to the page on
which that section begins. An asterisk indicates prayers
from section 2, "For the Very Young".

January

The last of the Christmas celebrations tips into
January, with the festival called Epiphany, which
recalls the visit of the wise men to the infant Jesus.

Winter themes are suitable for January, focusing
especially on the starkness and bareness of the month
and on severe weather and, unfortunately, the rise in
illness.

A key theme for the month is the new year, personal
resolutions to make a new start and new beginnings
of every kind.

February

The festival of Candlemas celebrates the time when the infant Jesus was taken to the temple by Mary and Joseph for a ceremony of thanksgiving and the old prophet Simeon declared that he was going to be "a light to reveal your will to the Gentiles". That may be why it was chosen as the time in some churches to bless the candles that were going to be used in the year ahead. The theme of light in the darkness is a good choice for the festival.

Candlemas   448
A New Day   11
The Elements   217

The season of Lent begins in February or March (depending on the date of Easter). It recalls the 40 days that Jesus spent in the wilderness thinking about the work that lay ahead of him.

The Season of Lent   449

Traditionally, for Christians, the first day of Lent is a special time for asking for God's forgiveness.

Forgiveness   399
Sorry and Confused   400
Wanting a New Start   406
Forgiving Others 414

The 40 days of Lent are a time when many Christians set aside extra time for Bible reading and prayer.

Following God   351
God in My Life   352
Inspiration from the Bible   368
Prayer   385
Hoping and Praying   386
Trusting in God   392

They are also a time for Christians to think about the needs of the world and what they should do to help.

March

Although Easter often falls in April rather than March, this is a good time for Christians to begin thinking about the events in Jesus' life leading up to Easter – the events from Palm Sunday to Good Friday sometimes known as Holy Week.

Mothering Sunday falls in Lent.

March is also the beginning of spring, and a time to be thinking about what will be growing in the countryside and in parks and gardens.

April

The events of Jesus' crucifixion and resurrection that Christians remember at Easter are at the heart of the Christian faith.

Holy Week   451
Easter   455

The joyful celebration of Jesus' resurrection can nevertheless be hard for anyone who has been recently bereaved, and linking the Easter theme to the promise of heaven can be helpful.

Hereafter   206

April and Easter are linked in popular imagination with flowers and baby animals.

Spring   237
Plants   248
Creatures Great and Small   255
Animals Around Us   256
Our World   44*

May

Forty days after Easter Christians remember Jesus going back to heaven. Ascension Day often falls in May.

Ascension, Pentecost and Trinity   462
Hereafter   206

May is also the first of the summer months that are so popular for weddings and baptisms.

Church Services and Celebrations   468

In schools, the summer term brings new interest to outdoor activities.

June

Fifty days after Easter Christians remember the coming of the Holy Spirit at Pentecost. The traditional church calendar then moves into the season called Trinity – the season for learning more about the God who is three in one: God the Father, God the Son and God the Holy Spirit.

Summer begins.

July

July brings the end of the school year.

July, like June, is a time for outdoor fun.

Friends   82
Things We Do   121
Sports   126
Outdoor Adventures   129
Out and About   39*

August

This is a very important month for the big holiday of the year, which might mean some very frustrating journeys as well as happy times.

Holidays 134
Outdoor Adventures 129
Courage and Patience on Journeys 139
Help Us Find Our Way 143

A holiday can be extra fun, but some young people feel unhappy about being away from home.

Thanks for the Day   476
Peace at Night   478
God Watch Over Me   488

Sometimes friends and family members can feel quite lonely when the people whom they usually rely on for company are away.

People I Love   71
Families   73
My Family   36*
Friends   82
Partings and Blessings   149

The time when school is out also gives more time for family activities.

Families   73
My Family   36*
All About Me   53
The Things of Every Day   63

September

September is a very popular months for harvest festivals. It is a time for celebration, but also a time for remembering those less fortunate.

Harvest   242
Plants   248
Bless Our Food   93
Famine and Disaster   318

September may also coincide with the start of the new school year.

At School   101
Out of School   105
Learning at School   106
Appreciating Learning   111
Difficult Times   113
Endings and Beginnings   120
Things We Do   121
Arts and Crafts   123
Sports   126
Friends   82
Out and About   39*
All About Me   53
Feeling Loved   54
Feeling Insecure   58
God by My Side   67

October

Harvest festivals continue into October, but this is also the month when autumn is at its most colourful.

Saint Francis Day is on 4 October. Because of the saint's love of creatures, schools and churches sometimes have services with a special focus on animals and birds.

Michaelmas actually falls in September, but thoughts of Michael and the angels provide a happy alternative to Hallowe'en traditions. Prayers of trust in God are also useful for anyone upset by the ghoulish focus of Hallowe'en customs.

November

Church traditions have chosen 1 November as
All Saints' Day and 2 November as All Souls. Even
Christians who do not have this tradition find it can
be helpful to set aside some time in the year to think
about those who have died and those who are left
bereaved.

Remembrance Day on 11 November may be marked
with prayers about death and dying. Other themes
for this day are to do with peace and forgiveness.

December

For many, December is all about Christmas. The
church season of Advent begins in late November,
but popularly on 1 December. It is a time for letting
go of the sorrows and mistakes in the past year and
looking forward to Christmas.

Advent   433
Forgiveness   399
A New Start   406
Everyday Sadness   165

Christmas is a time for celebrating the birth of Jesus.

Christmas   437
Peace   308

It is also a time for families and friends to enjoy
being together.

People I Love   71
Families   73
My Family   36*
Friends   82
Bless Our Home   88
Bless Our Food   93
Living as a Community   282

Prayers for winter and night-time also fit well with
the season's celebrations.

The Circle of the Year   232
Winter   235
Peace at Night   478
God Watch Over Me   488
God's Blessing   499
Good Night   50*

Index of First Lines

Please note that the number after each entry is the prayer number.

A

J

M

N

U

W

Y